Fortell Tarot Reading

TAROT SECRETS

Getting Straight to the Point

A definitive description of the Major and Minor Arcana cards

BENJAMIN CRABB

Printed in Australia

First Printing, 2023

ISBN: 978-0-6480806-7-1

Foretell Tarot

Dallas Vic 3047

www.fortelltarotreading.com

This book is dedicated to my mother Lucy.

About the Author

When I was a teenager, I remember hearing my mum shuffling her tarot cards as I walked up the hallway. Her tarot cards were so worn out you could barely see their pictures anymore. With her cigarette in her mouth, ashtray by her side and her TV, that she had since the 70's, switched on. I watched her shuffle, then quickly go through the deck and read them to herself, then she continued to shuffle again. I asked if she could read me my cards, and she passed them over to me. This was my very first time shuffling tarot cards, and it is where my interest in tarot cards began. I gave them back to my mum and she laid down 42 cards, 7 cards across and 6 rows down: a very in-depth and unique way of looking

Excitedly, I asked my mum what she saw in my cards. Her response was "You're going to meet someone." Lo and behold in the next few weeks, I did. That's when my interest turned into curiosity about how she knew that. I wanted to know where all the information came from.

My mum was a professional tarot card reader. I remember her reading for everyone; friends, family and clients that would come over to the house. Sadly, my mum stopped reading cards, she quit reading for everyone. The last time I saw her read was when she read for her mother. To this day I've never seen her read since; it's now been many years.

My interest in the tarot cards grew into a passion. I found it so fascinating how the cards were able to know what's happening, and how they were able to see and/or predict further ahead of time. I was so driven to know and learn how the tarot cards work and discover where they get all the information from with such pinpoint accuracy. The conclusion was our own energy.

As I continued to study and learn about the cards, my mum would often watch me in my element. I would lay out the cards and stare deeply into them. She would ask me "What do you see?" I would then begin to start explaining and showing her what I could see. She would then teach me how to group the cards and read them by putting them into a story formation. The next part was all up to me on how I translated and elaborated on what I saw and how I expressed the information. The more I kept practising the easier it became. I also looked for, and learned other ways to read the cards using different spreads.

I learned that the hardest person you could ever read for was yourself. The more you can see and know what's happening with yourself, the better you become at reading for others. To this day, I continue to practice and read for myself. It's an art that I believe you can never fully master, you will always continue to learn. The more you study, the more you're going to know.

As I continued to practise to sharpen and enhance my skills, I found myself teaching my mum new and different things that I had learnt and experienced as a professional tarot reader.

I have written this book not only to continue my mum's legacy and take over what she stopped doing, but also to share the passion I have in wanting to help others heal and move forward with their lives. To give them comfort, guidance, confirmation and reassurance.

This book is designed to be a foundational point into learning about all the major and minor cards of the tarot deck. It will help you understand all of the positive and negative aspects in straight to the point, basic details, with the easiest way to remember their meanings. Once you've learnt about both the positive and negative aspects of all the major and minor cards, then the reading process becomes easier.

CONTENTS

Getting Started

The most important, and fundamental rule of learning the tarot is not to rush. Learning about the tarot is a marathon, not a sprint race. The more time you invest in learning and having knowledge about each individual card, the better reader you'll become. When I was learning to read the tarot, I found that the easiest cards to learn about first was the Minor Arcana, by suit. This is due to their symbolical imagery. I believe it aids with giving you more definitions to the meaning of the card to its suit type. There are four suits, Cups, Swords, Pentacles and Wands.

The Major Arcana cards are more in-depth and have more hidden meanings in addition to their first impression meanings. When you start to combine more Major Arcana cards together, they can become more difficult to read in a spread. The Major Arcana cards overrule the Minors. The more Majors you have in a spread, the less control you have of the situation they are regarding and the influence and impact it will have. When your spread has a majority of Minor Arcana cards, you're likely to have more control of the situation, and have the ability to make sudden changes.

Always remember, every individual learns differently. I encourage you to spend as much time as possible. As you study them, it is important to see and feel what you believe that card is telling you. I suggest you don't overdo it. If you feel overwhelmed at any stage, simply put your cards down and walk away for a time. You don't want to overload yourself, and try to absorb everything all at once. This could lead to you forgetting more than you're learning.

Major Arcana Cards

Definitions:

Experiencing life-changing events which will have
long-term influences, Situations in which your destiny
is currently in control.

0. THE FOOL

CARD OF NEW BEGINNINGS

Positive Aspects

- New Beginnings
- Taking a leap of faith
- Living on the edge
- High energy
- Guided
- Carefree
- Dancer/ballet dancer - (Loves to dance)
- Well dressed - (Old fashioned but well presented)
- A short trip (Journey)
- Gaiety (Happiness)
- Can represent a gay male or female
- Taking a risk
- Fearless
- Clumsy person
- Good sense of humor
- A destination with mountains
- Living on a high - (In the moment)
- Dog lover/dog owner
- Person who has followers
- Warm destination by day but cold by night
- Travel
- The end of a situation
- New phase of life
- Innocence

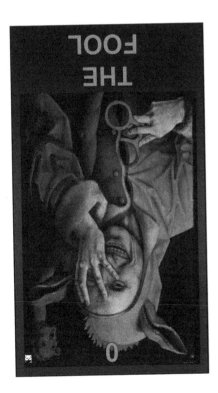

Negative Aspects

- Feeling foolish
- Look before you leap
- A copy cat
- Trying to be someone you're not
- Regret
- Too naïve
- Poor risk taking
- Foolish act
- Childish behaviour
- Danger ahead
- Carelessness
- Know your limits
- Dangerous mountains
- Areas of wild animals
- Too rushed
- Unprepared
- Stubbornness - (doesn't listen)
- Neglecting your dog and/or animals
- Outdated
- A know it all
- Poorly guided
- Untouchable
- Person has a lot going on in their mind
- Trying to make the right choice
- Feelings of making the wrong choice
- At the crossroads

1. THE MAGICIAN

CARD OF ORIGINALITY

POSITIVE ASPECTS

- Link between the higher realm and the physical realm
- A psychic mind reader
- A person who works in the field of magic
- A great problem solver
- A businessman - (Self employment)
- Entrepreneur
- Knows the tricks of the trades
- Highly skilled in all trades
- A tradesman and or handyman
- Knowing how to get out of tricky situations
- A person with a wealth of knowledge
- Guided by the divine
- A carpenter
- A candle maker - (He or she loves candles)
- Works with flowers and or in the garden
- A painter
- A hairdresser
- Well protected by the divine
- A religious type of person
- Good with their hands
- Starting a new project
- Willpower
- Very creative and artistic
- Someone who can manifest

NEGATIVE ASPECTS

- Skills used the wrong way
- Shifty handyman/tradesman
- Person who causes too many problems
- Trickery
- Con artist
- Uses their skills for revenge
- Lack of knowledge
- Master of illusions
- Plays mind games
- Manipulator
- He or she has a hidden agenda
- A psychic mind reader but won't reveal
- Someone who knows about you but won't reveal
- Two faced
- In and out type of person - (A quick fling in romance)
- Lack of willpower
- Lacks courage and skill
- Deceit
- Greed
- Unused ability
- Distrust
- Cunning
- Conniving
- Abuse of power

2. THE HIGH PRIESTESS

CARD OF BEAUTY AND KNOWLEDGE

POSITIVE ASPECTS

- Secrets revealed
- Good news revealed
- Revealing the truth
- Listening to, and following your intuition
- Psychic abilities
- Sticks to the good side - (The light)
- Heavily linked to the subconscious
- Someone in the field of calligraphy
- Nice hand writing
- A scroll collector or someone who is into scrolls
- Inner healing - Someone you can confide in
- Someone who has the same abilities as you
- A psychic
- Femininity
- Secret kept safe from a trustworthy source
- Trust your instincts
- Go with your gut feeling
- Hidden knowledge
- Desirability
- Mystery
- Subconscious
- Creativity
- Higher power
- Sensuality

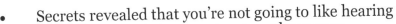

NEGATIVE ASPECTS

- Secrets revealed that you're not going to like hearing
- Revealing secrets to an untrustworthy source
- Doubt
- Too passive
- Doubting your psychic abilities
- Blocked Psyche
- Gossiper
- Spreading rumors and lies
- Using your secrets to expose you
- Person of bad influence
- Emotional blackmail
- Imbalance
- Psychic block
- Betrayal
- Mistake
- Ignorance
- Delusional
- Emotional imbalance
- Incorrect judgements
- Neediness
- Repression of intuition
- Unwanted attention
- Lack of self belief
- Uncontrolled outburst

3. THE EMPRESS
CARD OF PROMISE AND GROWTH

POSITIVE ASPECTS

- Mother figure
- Financial abundance
- Wealth
- Successful results
- Prosperity
- Birth
- Very attractive - The perfect physical look
- Small hips, big breasts, hour glass hip features
- Tall woman
- Can represent your partner - (Especially if you're married)
- Someone who is middle aged of 40 and over
- Beautiful hair
- Admired by lots of men and women
- Loves nature and her garden
- Sensitive and empathetic
- Fruit lover
- The perfect mother
- News in relation to a pregnancy
- Goddess type
- Great lover
- Caretaker
- Success in business
- Nurturing
- Creativity
- Affection

NEGATIVE ASPECTS

- A mother who neglects her child/children
- Miscarriage
- Uses her beauty to get out of trouble
- A strutter
- Uses her body for money
- Lust not love
- Loss of abundance
- Unsuccessful results
- Unsuccessful in business
- An immature age and/or older woman
- An ex wife
- Overprotective
- Problems with pregnancy
- An unwanted pregnancy
- Unsupportive female
- Insecurity
- Infertility
- Lack of confidence
- Overbearing tendencies
- Disharmony
- Negligence
- Clinginess
- Dependence
- Creative blockages

16

4. THE EMPEROR

CARD OF WORLDLY POWER

POSITIVE ASPECTS

- Father figure
- A powerful man
- In a powerful position
- You have the power
- Wisdom
- Middle aged man normally over 50
- Knows a lot about life
- Grandfather figure
- Wealth of experience
- Long life
- Authority
- Promotion
- Leadership
- Hard worker
- Discipline
- Self-control
- Strength and success
- Achieving a level of status
- Rise of power
- Powerful people have an interest in you
- Recognition
- Stability
- Dependability
- Protectiveness

NEGATIVE ASPECTS

- Conflicted
- Resentment
- Denied responsibility
- Petty rules and regulations
- Complications with your father/grandfather
- Abusing power
- Stubbornness
- Power struggles
- Lack of discipline
- Unsuccessful
- Demotion
- Failed ambitions
- Untrustworthy
- Immaturity
- Lack of power and authority
- Excessive controlling
- Rigidity
- Lack of control
- Absent father
- Paternity/father
- Severity
- Inflexibility
- Aggression
- Punishment

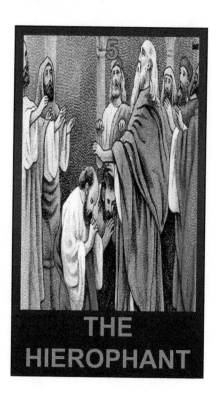

5. THE HIEROPHANT

CARD OF ORTHODOXY

POSITIVE ASPECTS

- Disciplined
- Teacher
- Preacher
- Counsellor
- Great speaker
- Public speaking
- Solid organization
- Community
- Class
- Great listener
- Old traditional values
- Long term commitments
- Success
- A following
- Wealth of knowledge
- Wealth of experience
- Pope
- Ceremony
- Priest
- Religious man
- Strong relationships
- Marriage
- Great advice
- Forgiveness
- Church

NEGATIVE ASPECTS

- Short term commitments
- Cult leader
- Failed marriage
- Man made laws
- Stubborn and exasperating person
- Unsuccessful
- Unforgiving
- Non committed
- Poor advice
- Teaching bad examples
- Cult organization
- Knowledge and wisdom used the wrong way
- Bad influences
- Negative preaching
- Lack of knowledge
- Uninspired
- Outdated tradition
- Judgement for lifestyle
- Being punished for doing the right thing
- Nonconformity
- Reject authority
- Alternative lifestyles
- Reversed roles
- Relationship problems

6. THE LOVERS

CARD OF CHOICE

POSITIVE ASPECTS

- New love
- New relationship
- New romance
- A change
- Making a physical change
- True love
- Destined for love
- A love with a blessing
- Perfect harmony
- For a man - (Knows that she's the one)
- For a woman - (Questions the relationship but makes her decision with caution)
- Trusting relationship
- Model - nudist
- Someone who likes to skinny dip
- Relationship guided by the divine
- Strong relationship
- Strong chemistry
- Unity
- Passion
- An opportunity
- A specific lover
- Re emergence of an old relationship
- Strong physical connection
- Passionate feelings

NEGATIVE ASPECTS

- Temptation
- Lust
- Physical attraction only
- Affairs
- Infidelity
- Obsession instead of passion
- Toxic relationship
- Resisting the temptation to change
- The wrong path
- A prostitute
- Lack of sexual chemistry
- Missed opportunity
- One sided relationship controlled by the male
- Dominating male in the relationship
- Disharmony
- Trust issues
- Insecurity
- Imbalance
- Disconnection
- Lack of accountability
- Disunion
- Detachment
- Bad decisions made
- Misalignment

7. THE CHARIOT

CARD OF MIND CONTROL

POSITIVE ASPECTS

- Victory
- Triumphant
- A vehicle and/or a new vehicle
- Someone in control of their lives and themselves
- An ordeal/past troubles have been overcome
- Movement
- Change
- An improvement in health
- Inner strength
- Drive and willpower
- Ambition
- Courage
- Overcoming conflicts
- Well protected
- Overcoming tough obstacles
- Determination
- Motivated
- Ambitious
- Success in sports and competitions
- Recognition
- Fame and fortune
- Inspiration
- Being an authority
- Travel - mainly by car
- Confident

NEGATIVE ASPECTS

- Inner conflict
- Problems with a vehicle
- A war
- Conflict
- Tough obstacles ahead
- A lack of drive
- Problems with health
- Desire for revenge
- Lack of will power
- No direction
- No control
- Aggression
- Lack of courage
- Someone with bad influences around you
- A bully
- Selfish
- Delays regarding travel
- Rushing into a relationship
- Lack of direction
- Forcefulness
- Lack of self control
- Powerlessness
- Instability
- Using others for your benefit

8. STRENGTH

CARD OF COURAGE

POSITIVE ASPECTS

- Patience
- A very patient person
- Healing
- Someone who has great physical strength
- Someone with strong hands
- Fearless
- Self control
- Endurance
- Courage
- Determination
- Great faith
- Confidence
- A calm, tactful and wise approach to problems should be sought
- Self-disciplined
- Overcoming problems
- Strength from the divine
- Good and/or improved health
- Inner strength
- Zoo keeper - someone who works with dangerous animals
- Spiritual healing
- Someone who likes to meditate and/or attends a mediation class
- Connecting to the divine

NEGATIVE ASPECTS

- Lack of willpower
- Impatient
- Delays
- Too much fear
- Lack of faith
- Someone with weak hands
- Lack of physical strength
- Too rushed
- A very impatient person
- Problems with health
- Lack of faith
- Vulnerability
- Problems connecting to the divine
- Someone who quits too easily
- A victim of bullying
- Self doubt
- Undisciplined
- Lack of confidence
- Weakness
- Lack of inner strength
- Feeling helpless
- Lack of self-control
- Low self-esteem
- Feeling inadequate

9. THE HERMIT

CARD OF WISDOM

POSITIVE ASPECTS

- Soul searching
- Spending time alone
- Someone who has chosen to be on his or her own
- Waiting
- Someone who loves to be in the dark
- Studying - (In the field of teaching)
- Seeing the light at the end of the tunnel
- Centering oneself
- Someone who enjoys their own company
- A cold place
- Independence
- Solitariness
- Reassessing
- Taking time out to think
- Finding something that has been lost
- Making new friends
- The return of confidence
- Someone who is single
- Coming out of your comfort zone
- Spiritual enlightenment
- Self reflection
- Inner guidance
- Wisdom
- Introspection
- Patience

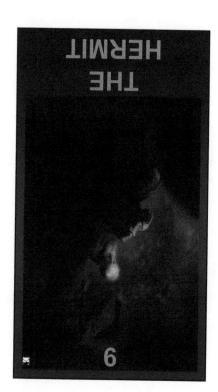

NEGATIVE ASPECTS

- Can't see the light
- A job that you dislike - (Always checking the time)
- A waste of time
- Delay
- Slow movement
- Ignoring offers of help
- Loneliness
- Exclusion
- Isolated
- Self-pity
- Dwelling on what has been lost
- Reluctant to accept new ideas
- Lack of responsibility for oneself
- Homeless
- Living in the past
- Low on confidence
- Rejection
- Paranoia
- Withdrawal
- Antisocial
- Restrictive
- A lack of communication
- Rejection
- Alienation

10. WHEEL OF FORTUNE

CARD OF CHANGE PROGRESSING

THE WHEEL OF FORTUNE

POSITIVE ASPECTS

- Positive change
- Luck is on your side
- Karmic balance
- Someone who works in a library
- Someone who owns a bookshop business
- Stroke of good fortune
- New beginnings
- Ending of a love affair and getting knowledge from it
- Destined change
- Good things are repeated
- Positive results
- Author
- Book lover
- Destiny and fate in your favour
- A windfall
- Soulmates
- Outcomes in your favour
- Change for the best
- Success and achievement
- Travel
- An act of dharma
- Fated change
- Decisive moments
- Cycles of life
- Happy events

THE WHEEL OF FORTUNE

NEGATIVE ASPECTS

- Run of bad luck
- Going around in circles
- Not your turn
- External forces
- Delays
- Setbacks
- Unwelcome change
- What goes up must come down
- Quick change for the worst
- Out of control
- Warning
- An act of karma
- Cancellations
- Vulnerable
- Misfortune
- What goes around, comes around
- Stuck in a rut
- Failure
- Loss
- Fraud
- Upheaval
- Disorder
- Disruption
- Resistance to change

11. JUSTICE

CARD OF HONESTY

POSITIVE ASPECTS

- Balance in your favour
- The act of justice
- A karmic balance
- A judge
- Law and order
- A lawyer
- Seeking legal advice
- In control
- Speaking the truth
- Honesty
- Power
- The right decision has been made
- Learning from past experiences
- Legal matters
- Doing what you think is best
- Self-satisfaction in accomplishments
- Fairness
- Avoiding prison
- Community services
- Commitment
- Signing legal documentation
- Court cases
- Contracts
- Positive legal outcomes
- Cause and effect

NEGATIVE ASPECTS

- Injustice
- Bias
- Prison sentence
- Unfairness
- Lies
- Lack of power
- Not in control
- Negative legal outcomes
- Negative commitments
- Signing illegal documentation
- Getting what you deserve for the worst
- Fake or fraud contracts
- Controversies
- Confrontations
- Serious disputes
- Karmic retribution
- Dishonesty
- Corruption
- Lack of accountability
- Divorce
- Abuse of power and status
- Extremism
- Conviction
- Defeat

12. THE HANGED MAN

CARD OF SACRIFICE

POSITIVE ASPECTS

- Freedom
- Breaking away from stagnation
- On the move again
- Gaining more knowledge
- Increased studying - University
- Working on spiritual development
- A lot happening behind closed doors
- Stagnation made by choice
- Short and temporary delays
- Sacrificing one thing to gain another
- Clearing out the old, making way for something new
- Sacrifices
- Taking time out to make a decision
- Change
- Time to be out on your own
- Unexpected change at home or work
- Movement and growth in different directions
- Someone who works in a circus, doing stunts and acrobatics
- Transitioning
- Psychic abilities
- Enlightened
- Patience
- Clairvoyance

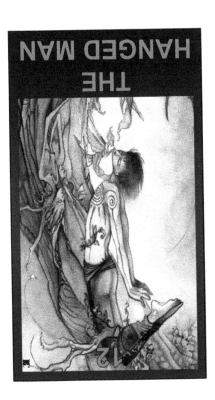

NEGATIVE ASPECTS

- Unhappy situation
- Stuck in a rut
- Uncertainty over which path to take
- Failing to commit to long term studies
- Long delays
- Too much stagnation in your life
- Suicide
- Ill health
- Prison sentence
- Imprisonment
- Useless sacrifices
- Waiting for nothing
- Unwilling to make sacrifices
- Self-inflicted torture
- Playing the game
- Lack of direction in love, career and life
- Discontentment
- Apathy
- Disinterest
- Impulsiveness
- Detachment
- Insecurity
- Lack of spiritual growth
- Deception

13. DEATH

CARD OF TRANSFORMATION

POSITIVE ASPECTS

- Transitioning
- New beginnings
- The end of a phase
- Rebirth
- Change
- Something that's coming to an end
- Peace
- Tranquility
- Leaving the past behind you
- Spiritual transformation
- Opportunities
- The right time, a blessing in disguise
- Life changing events
- Clearing out old habits
- Passing from one phase to another
- The ending of a mishap
- Death of your old self
- Situations coming to an end
- A new life
- The beginning of a new era
- Creation
- End of a cycle
- Resolving
- Spiritual transformation
- Moving forward

NEGATIVE ASPECTS

- Death
- Sudden
- Traumatic
- Shock
- Resisting change
- A Funeral
- Fear of psychical death
- Grieving
- Depression
- Divorce
- Inevitable endings
- Difficulties in handling the change
- Debt
- Warning against speeding or parking cars illegally
- Loss of income and or financial security
- Beware of the law
- In limbo
- Delayed change
- Fears
- Darkness
- Repeating of bad habits
- Lessons not learnt
- An ending of a relationship/partnership
- Danger of accidents

14. TEMPERANCE

CARD OF TO EXPLORE IN MODERATION

POSITIVE ASPECTS

- Period of busyness
- Finding the right balance
- Someone who works with drinks - (Bartender, Barista)
- Expanding your horizons
- Peace and harmony
- Good management
- Contentment
- Peaceful home life
- Balancing your emotions
- Someone with strong emotional energy
- Growth
- Testing the waters
- Success
- Period of calmness
- In control
- Patience
- Trying new things
- Someone who is a drink tester - (Wine, Beer, Coffee)
- Compassion
- Cooperation
- Good composure
- Well balanced partnership
- Setting goals
- The ability to combine and balance
- Maintaining your present security

NEGATIVE ASPECTS

- Unwilling to compromise
- Impatience
- Sloppiness
- Imbalanced
- Imbalanced emotions
- Emotional baggage
- Someone who drinks excessively
- Taking on too much
- Health problems - (from lower waist down)
- Lack of compassion
- Poor composer
- A lack of cooperation
- Too one sided in a relationship
- An unbalanced relationship and/or partnership
- Hectic times ahead
- Burning candles at both ends
- Over indulgence
- Moodiness
- Uncertainty
- Hastiness
- Recklessness
- Lack of perspective
- Overlooking obvious problems
- Poor choices

15. THE DEVIL

CARD OF BONDAGE

POSITIVE ASPECTS

- Commitment
- Breaking free
- Tied into a situation
- Acceptance of a very difficult situation
- Sexual attraction
- Strong desire
- The drive to make things happen
- Having the ability to influence others
- Freedom from restraints
- Breaking from substances and/or addiction
- Letting go of fear
- Confronting inner fears and anxieties
- Creating a healthier diet and/or lifestyle
- Quitting of bad habits - (Drinking, Smoking)
- Seeking professional help
- Detachment
- Revelation
- Spiritual awakening
- Self-discipline
- Responsibility
- Reclaiming control
- Hard work
- Liberation
- Defeat
- Reclaiming power

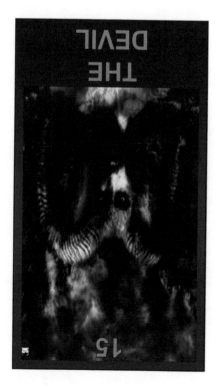

NEGATIVE ASPECTS

- Obsessions
- Temptations
- Lust
- Sexual desires, and/or passion used the wrong way
- Anger
- Crimes
- Violence
- Self-punishment
- Developing an unhealthy attachment to someone or something
- Substance problems or abuse
- Addictions problems or abuse
- A possession
- Greedy
- Inconsiderate
- Bondage
- Over indulgence
- Abuse
- Cruel intentions
- Psychological torture
- Manipulation
- Divorce
- Dark thoughts
- Hiding your deepest and darkest self from others

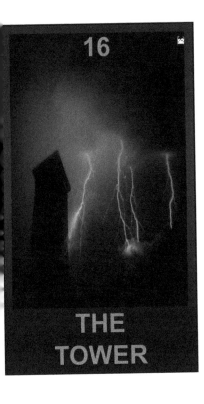

16. THE TOWER
CARD OF AWAKENING

POSITIVE ASPECTS

- Sudden change for the better
- A surprise
- Unexpected outcomes in your favour
- A shock
- An idea
- Rebuilding
- New beginning
- Enlightenment can lead to freedom
- Someone who works on, or owns a lighthouse
- Misfortunes are a blessing in disguise
- A sudden change of attitude
- Physical and passionate releases
- Serendipity
- Rebuilding broken relationship/s and/or partnership/s
- Quick decisions
- Fast moving projects
- A breakthrough
- Someone who works with electricity - electrician or works in the field of electricity
- Someone who works on buildings
- Relationship with sparks and lost of energy
- Revelation
- An awakening
- Someone who likes skydiving and/or jumping from heights

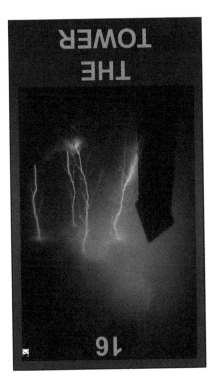

NEGATIVE ASPECTS

- Failure
- Loss
- Catastrophe
- Divorce
- Suicidal thoughts and tendencies
- A shocking ending
- Struck by psychical lightening
- Financial losses
- Aggression - (Violent upheaval)
- Breakdown in relationship/s and/or partnership/s
- Pressure building up in the mind and exploding
- Someone' who self-destructs
- Surround by violence
- Problems with house structures and or foundations
- Loss of power
- Electrical problems with building/s
- Fatal accident
- Sudden change for the worse
- Someone who is suffering from shock
- Resisting change
- Bankruptcy
- Chaos
- Natural disasters
- Revelations

17. THE STAR

CARD OF TRUTH

POSITIVE ASPECTS

- High hopes
- Wishes fulfilled
- Faith
- Making a wish
- Near future
- Hope for the future
- Inspiration
- Motivated
- Spiritual connection
- In tune with the universe
- Dreams fulfilled
- Improvements
- Getting what you want
- Soulmate
- Destiny
- Opportunity
- Renewal
- Calm
- Serenity
- Healing
- Creativity
- Future goals
- Improved health
- Promising opportunities
- Solid foundations

NEGATIVE ASPECTS

- Not getting what you want
- False hopes
- Jealousy
- Theft
- Wishes unfulfilled
- Aiming too high
- Emotionally distant
- Delays
- Blocked energies
- Hopelessness
- Despair
- Lack of faith
- Boredom
- Lack of inspiration
- Focusing on the negative
- Lack of creativity
- Feeling anxious and overwhelmed
- Lack of confidence
- Monotony
- Human nervous system out of order
- Disconnection
- Doubt
- Anxiety
- Insecurity

18. THE MOON

CARD OF EMOTIONS

POSITIVE ASPECTS

- Subconscious
- Psychic abilities
- Beginning of psychic developments
- Time to clear the air
- Coming out of the dark and having a go
- Noticing your dream
- Building your own security
- An unfoldment of your conscious
- Guided by your intuition
- Revealing the truth
- Emotionally sensitive
- Someone who dreams a lot
- Psychic dreams
- A period of confusion will come to an end soon
- Confiding in a friend
- Revealing a secret
- Mysterious
- Creativity
- Femininity
- All is not as bad as you think
- Welcoming cycles
- Intuition
- An ending of problems
- Artistic and creative
- Someone who works in movies or the arts field

NEGATIVE ASPECTS

- Confusion
- Depression
- Deception
- Fears
- Phobias
- Despair
- Inability to face problems
- Illusions
- Lies and mysteries
- Self-delusion
- Uncontrollable emotions
- Negative emotions
- Loneliness
- Lack of direction
- Hopelessness
- Fears in the mind
- Down in debts
- Insecurities
- Jealousy
- Muddled feelings
- Bad energy
- Danger
- False friends
- Infidelity

19. THE SUN

CARD OF HAPPINESS AND FREEDOM

POSITIVE ASPECTS

- Happiness
- Contentment
- Good news
- Freedom
- Promising relationship/s
- Success
- In control of situations at the present time
- A new life
- Successful marriage
- Going outside of boundaries
- Growth of personal wealth
- New ventures will prosper
- A good summer ahead
- Good health
- Travel - (A warm destination)
- A young boy
- Peace
- Optimism
- Personal achievements
- High energy
- Achieving goals
- Birth
- Joy
- Productivity
- Abundance

NEGATIVE ASPECTS

- Too naive
- Blind to the truth
- Daydreaming
- Disillusionment
- Problems regarding a child or children
- Experiencing difficulties becoming pregnant
- Lack of enthusiasm
- Sadness
- Unsuccessful marriage
- Feeling unloved
- Impatient
- Unsuccessful relationship and/or partnership
- Unachieved
- Losses
- Unhappiness
- Not in control of current situation
- Delays in travel
- Destination with drought
- Pessimism
- Still birth
- Abortion
- Oppression
- Childish attitude
- False pride

20. JUDGEMENT

CARD OF TRANSFORMING OPENESS

POSITIVE ASPECTS

- Good judgement
- Making the right decision
- An announcement
- Peace
- Musician - (Flute)
- Standing ovation
- A calling
- Good news
- An awakening
- Recognizing your positive and negatives
- Seeing where you're currently at
- Legal matters
- Coming to terms with the truth
- The final settlement of a matter
- A decision has been made
- Letting go of the past
- Fate steps in
- You are being watched
- Evaluated
- Transformation
- Life changing
- A reckoning
- Self-evaluation
- Forgiveness
- Composure

NEGATIVE ASPECTS

- Loss of opportunity
- Not in control of the outcomes
- Not meant to be
- Self-doubt
- Lack of awareness
- Failing to learn lessons
- Self-loathing
- Poor judgment
- Self-denying
- A burden
- Repeating the same mistakes
- Unwillingness to learn
- Karmic lessons
- False accusations
- Unfair
- Gossiping
- Indecisiveness
- An inner critic
- Ignoring the call
- Delays
- Regrets
- Weakness
- Loss of income
- Indecision

21. THE WORLD

CARD OF SUCCESS

POSITIVE ASPECTS

- Freedom
- Travel - (The world, Overseas)
- Self-discipline
- Free to go in any direction
- Success
- Wisdom
- Growth
- Healing
- Changes
- Completing studies
- Accepting new responsibilities
- Moving out of home
- Totally balanced
- Expanding your horizons
- Good vibrations
- Making others happy
- Completion
- Spiritual wholeness
- Completion of a cycle
- Successful completion of a project
- Ending of one cycle/phase in life
- A new cycle
- Fulfilment
- Worldly success
- Ready to move on

NEGATIVE ASPECTS

- Recurring problems
- Travel delays
- Delays
- Delayed completion
- Stuck in a rut
- Frustration
- Unable to break free
- Boredom
- Obstacles ahead
- Restriction to go in any place
- Lack of self discipline
- Unbalanced
- Unsuccessful
- Lack of freedom
- Impatience
- Negative cycle
- Learning too little
- Taking the easy way out - (Half hearted efforts)
- Stagnation
- Isolation
- Incomplete
- Burden
- A new beginning not welcomed
- Lack of progress

Minor Arcana Cards

Definitions:

Dealing with day-to-day issues which will not
necessarily have a lasting influence on your life.
These issues are passing through, presenting you
with an opportunity to learn from these experiences,
Situations in which you are in control with.

CUPS

ELEMENT: Water
STAR SIGNS: Pisces, Cancer and Scorpio.
SEASON: Summer
UNITS OF TIME: Weeks or Days
ACE OF CUPS: Approximately 1 week

BRIEF DESCRIPTIONS:

Cups represent: emotions, love, expressing of feelings, relationships and connections, emotions in relation to others, friendships, heart rules the head, creativity, fantasy, imagination, romance, passion, conscious and subconscious feelings, getting in touch with your emotions, contentment, wish fulfillment, family happiness, love of life, and nostalgia

ACE OF CUPS

CARD OF EMOTIONAL EXPERIENCE

POSITIVE ASPECTS

- Emotional fulfillment and contentment
- New/existing lover
- Passion
- New beginning
- Emotion
- Love
- The beginning of a good friendship or work association
- Affection
- Romance
- Marriage
- The beginning of a new relationship
- A lovely gift - (A ring)
- Peace
- A great social life
- The awakening of talents
- Artistic nature
- Learning to love oneself
- Someone who gives a lot of love
- The beginning of an emotional experience
- Good health
- Abundance
- The beginning of an inspirational period in life
- A new home
- Celebrations
- Fertility

NEGATIVE ASPECTS

- Sadness
- Loneliness
- Disappointment
- Friendship rather than love
- The ending of a love affair
- Lack of love
- Unhappy relationship and/or partnership
- Depression
- Emotionally unstable
- Lack of empathy
- Someone who cries too much
- Problems with water
- A breakup
- Problems with old memories
- Pain
- Health problems - (Kidneys)
- Lack of emotion
- Bad news
- Sensitive to stress
- Too vulnerable in love
- Unwanted pregnancy
- Over indulging
- Lack of progression
- Cancellation of celebrations

2 OF CUPS

CARD OF HEALING

POSITIVE ASPECTS

- Love
- Friendship
- Marriage
- An engagement
- A loving relationship and/or friendship
- Good colleagues
- Happy work atmosphere
- Someone special in your life who you are fond of
- A love affair
- An end of a rivalry with another person
- A supportive friendship
- Male and female effort and understanding
- A trustworthy relationship
- Happy relationship and/or partnership
- A great business partnership
- An end of a disagreement with another person
- A friendship of equals
- Mutual forgiveness
- Tolerance
- A gift of some sort
- Harmony
- A healing relationship
- Exchanging good ideas
- A joyous event
- Connecting

NEGATIVE ASPECTS

- A parting
- Misunderstandings
- Ending an engagement
- Separation
- Quarrels
- Divorce
- Someone who needs healing
- Conflict
- Problems with a relationship and/or partnership
- Breaking an agreement
- Clash of personalities
- Too focused on each other
- Fear of commitment
- Spending too much time together
- Excluding other people
- Initial attraction state
- Stuck
- A relationship that burns out quickly
- Too one sided
- Relationship and/or partnership that never leaves the beginning stages
- Too much giving, and not enough receiving
- Imbalance
- Incompatibility

3 OF CUPS

CARD OF CELEBRATIONS

POSITIVE ASPECTS

- Celebration
- Artistic and creative projects
- A wedding
- New clothes/well dressed
- A marriage
- Growth
- Birth
- The birth of good ideas
- A birthday
- Parties
- Abundance
- A gathering
- Happiness
- Contentment
- Dance class
- Good fortune
- Good family life
- Spiritual growth
- Good news
- Group
- An engagement
- Christening or some type of blessing
- Beginning of a new lifestyle
- New clothes
- A business in the clothing industry

NEGATIVE ASPECTS

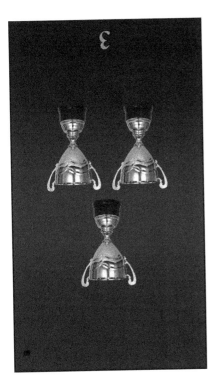

- Selfishness
- Exploitation
- Domestic problems
- Divorce
- 3 is a crowd - (Someone interfering with a situation)
- Lack of generosity
- Broken engagements
- Dishonesty amongst a group
- Gossiping
- Betrayal
- Delayed celebration
- Taking advantage of people
- Nothing to celebrate
- Period of waiting
- Cancelled wedding
- Problems with family
- Over self-indulgence
- Bad news or false company of friends in your circle
- Treachery
- Lack of a social life
- Cheating
- Miscarriage
- Termination
- Envy

4 OF CUPS

CARD OF HIDDEN WISDOM

POSITIVE ASPECTS

- An offer
- An opportunity
- New friends
- Growth
- An idea
- Resisting temptation
- A surprise
- Something out of nothing
- Lost then found
- Something new to look forward too
- Gratitude
- Seeking help
- New interests
- Letting go of regret
- An end of stagnation
- Proactive
- Positive attitude
- Re-energized
- Motivated to make a change
- Emotional stability
- Loyalty
- Sticking it out to the end
- Reliability
- Safety
- Gratitude

NEGATIVE ASPECTS

- Boredom
- Depression
- Self indulgence
- Apathy
- Dissatisfaction
- The grass isn't always greener over the hill
- Feeling of something missing
- Stuck in a rut
- Lack of variety
- Taking good fortune for granted
- Dejection
- Self-pity
- Drinking and/or eating excessively
- Problems with drugs and or alcohol
- Don't know what you want
- Contemplation
- Dreaming of the past
- Carelessness
- Emotionally introverted
- Lack of motivation
- Indecisive
- Regret
- Refusing offers
- Lack of excitement

5 OF CUPS

CARD OF SORROW

POSITIVE ASPECTS

- Not all is lost
- An inheritance
- Large sums of money
- Making the most of what you have left
- Healing
- Accepting what is
- Moving on
- Rebuilding your life
- The situation is not as bad as what it seems
- Taking back control of your emotions
- Appreciation of what good is left
- Positive thinking
- A learning experience
- Rekindling of old relationship/friendship
- A warning
- Someone who is empathetic
- Learning from your mistakes
- Overcoming despair
- Someone who is compassionate
- Valuable experience learned
- Self forgiveness
- Personal setbacks
- Asking for help
- Confiding in others
- Crying over spilt milk

NEGATIVE ASPECTS

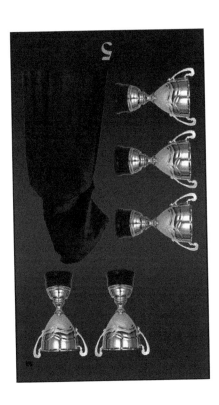

- Loss
- Sadness
- Disappointment
- Remorse
- Mourning
- Grieving
- Feeling miserable
- Downhearted
- Wondering whether to walk away or not
- A breakup in relationship/friendship
- Dissatisfied
- Divorce
- Emotional instability
- Negative thinking
- Absence
- Emotional fear
- Self pity
- Suffering
- Separation
- Tears
- Death
- Depression
- Loneliness
- Focusing on the losses only

6 OF CUPS
CARD OF PAST MEMORIES

POSITIVE ASPECTS

- Past memories of happy times
- Childhood
- A gift with lots of love - (Flowers)
- Looking through old photos/photo albums
- Someone who likes or works in the field of photography
- The past coming back to the present
- Someone who works in the field of teaching - (A school teacher)
- Young children
- Someone who works with flowers - (A florist/gardener)
- Renewing an interest from the past
- Someone from the past has come back into your life
- A hobby and/or business
- Reviving something from the past
- Solving present problems by looking back at the past
- A family gathering
- Old skills resurrected for the future
- Old friends
- Children may soon become very important
- An act of kindness
- Sharing
- Creativity
- Known joy
- Moving out of home
- Homesickness

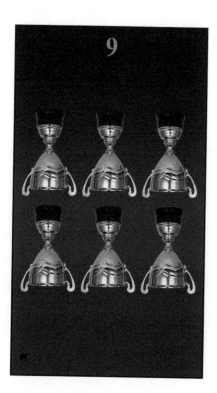

NEGATIVE ASPECTS

- Living in the past
- Unhappy memories
- Regret about good times gone by
- The past repeating itself
- Nostalgia
- Puppy love only
- Child like behavior
- Unable to accept the past
- Friendship only
- Child abuse
- Stagnation
- Not living in the moment
- Guilt
- Anxiety
- Too much giving and not enough receiving
- Outdated ideas and prospects
- A bad childhood
- Boredom
- Lack of creativity
- Unforgiving
- Seeking revenge for past actions
- Trauma
- Clinging to the past
- Repeating negative patterns

7 OF CUPS

CARD OF CHOICES AND BIG DECISIONS

POSITIVE ASPECTS

- Opportunities
- Making the right choice
- Choosing wisely
- Fantasy
- Choices
- New ideas
- Hopes and aspirations
- Big decisions
- Reaching out for your dream
- Taking all you can
- Wealth
- Gifts
- Victory
- An adventure
- Wisdom
- Intuition
- Wishful thinking
- Meditation
- New projects
- Creativity
- Visions
- New options
- Ambitions
- Determination
- Desires

NEGATIVE ASPECTS

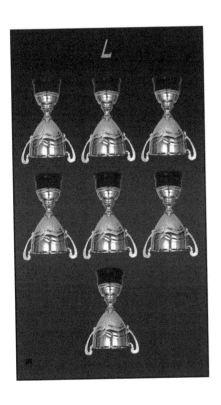

- Delusion
- Fantasy
- Bewilderment
- Day dreaming
- Muddle and confusion
- Too many options to choose from
- Ego
- Imaginations
- Scattered energies
- Fears
- Difficulties in making decision/s
- A reality check
- Confusion
- Lack of clarity
- Fear of making a poor choices
- Disappointment
- Lack of choices
- Immaturity
- Missed opportunities
- Living in fantasy world
- Temptations
- Instability
- Escapism
- Avoiding issues

8 OF CUPS

CARD OF AWARENESS

POSITIVE ASPECTS

- Moving on
- Seeking new adventures
- Searching for deeper meaning in life
- Walking away from an emotional situation
- Go for what your worth
- Wanting to do something different
- Personal development
- New beginnings
- New relationship/s and or friendship/s
- An ending of a bad time
- Emotional stability
- Celebrations
- New projects
- Moving house
- New job
- Taking risks
- Friends who offer support and assistance
- Changes to lifestyle
- Searching for your inner self
- Spirituality
- Passion
- Attraction
- Achievements
- Walking into happiness
- Effort

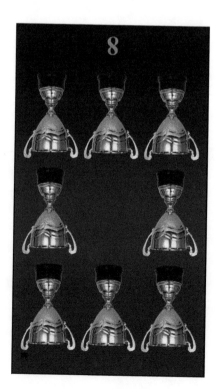

NEGATIVE ASPECTS

- Emotional discontent
- Needing more
- Something missing in your life
- Walking away from relationship/friendship
- Feeling something is missing
- Abandonment
- Leaving everything behind
- Bad times will continue for a while
- Lack of peace and security
- A bad mistake
- Taking risks that turn out to be a fantasy
- Greedy
- Regret
- Feeling guilty
- Abandoning friends and or family
- Overestimated
- Evasion
- Anger
- Deception
- Insecurity
- Stagnation
- Faking happiness
- Depression
- Loneliness

9 OF CUPS

THE WISH CARD

POSITIVE ASPECTS

- Wish fulfillment
- Feasting
- Contentment
- Happiness
- Hospitality
- Satisfaction
- Pleasure
- Marriage
- Love
- Friendship
- Good company
- Comfortable surroundings
- Companionship with family and friends
- Security
- Confident
- Good health
- Material gain
- Accomplishment
- Achievement
- A collector
- Prosperity
- Success
- Rewards
- Celebration
- Abundance

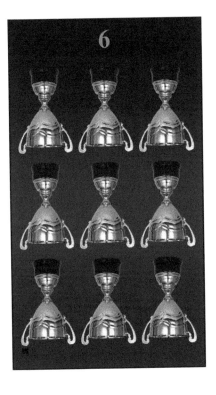

NEGATIVE ASPECTS

- Complacency
- Superficiality
- Smugness
- Over confident
- Egoism
- Self-centered
- Laziness
- Greedy
- Self-indulgence
- Dissatisfaction
- Lack of goals and ambition
- Disappointment
- Unhappiness
- Underachievement
- Arrogance
- Eating disorders/addictions
- Misery
- Wishes unfulfilled
- Shattered dreams
- Misery
- Self-hatred
- Nightmares

10 OF CUPS

CARD OF CONTENTMENT

POSITIVE ASPECTS

- Family Happiness
- Contentment
- The weekend
- Marriage security
- Emotional stability
- Happy children
- Marriage
- Peace
- Prosperity
- Experiencing the state of happiness you desire
- Things are suddenly happening
- Exciting vibrations
- Fulfilment
- Lasting relationships
- A new home
- Perfect relationships
- Fairytale ending
- Perfect harmony
- Family gatherings
- Domestic bliss
- Family reunions
- Soulmates
- Balance
- Abundance of love and support
- Achievement

NEGATIVE ASPECTS

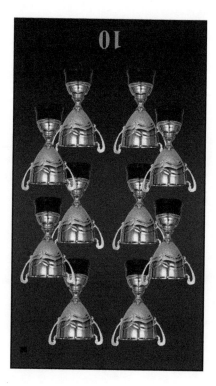

- Disrupted happiness
- A disgruntled individual
- Disharmony
- Lack of security
- Social services
- Lack of stability
- Homesick
- Divorce
- Abandoning children
- Neglect
- Abuse
- Miscarriage
- Violence
- Dysfunctional family
- Cold feet
- A break-up
- Emotional problems
- Resentment
- Broken home
- Infertility
- A short fling
- Isolation
- Hostile workplace
- Arguments with family over finances

PAGE OF CUPS

CARD OF IMAGINATION

POSITIVE ASPECTS

- A child or young person
- Someone who is very caring
- Something great happening to this person
- An experienced person
- A gentle and quiet person
- Someone who studies dreams
- Training, education or teaching
- Someone who is very sensitive
- A situation that turns out well
- Keeps emotions under control
- People who are artistic
- Ready to start a new project
- Beginning of a learning situation
- Day dreaming
- An admirer
- Emotional
- Good News
- Shyness
- Romantic
- Announcement
- Birth
- Messages
- Love
- Affection
- Creativity

NEGATIVE ASPECTS

- A lazy frivolous person
- Someone who neglects to use their skills and talents
- Drifting from one activity to another
- Someone who fails to make a commitment to anything
- Achieving very little
- Wasted potential
- Underdeveloped artistic, creative or psychic talents
- A help situation that has been overlooked
- Ignorance coming from the unconscious mind
- Repressed Feelings
- Exaggeration
- Lack of stability
- Self-pity
- Confliction and deception
- A childish behavior approach
- Lives in a fantasy world
- Seduction
- Childhood issues
- Broken dreams
- Bad news
- Obsession
- Broken promises
- Vulnerability
- Envy

KNIGHT OF CUPS
CARD OF PROPOSAL

POSITIVE ASPECTS

- A very sensitive caring person
- An intelligent person
- Romantic person/Prince Charming
- A lover coming into your life
- An invitation/Something being offered
- Someone in search of an ideal
- Following a dream
- Setting out on a journey
- Coming or going of a matter
- Someone going out to the field of service
- All things are flowing through slow and steady
- A young man may offer interesting invitations or proposals
- Indulges in fantasy rather than apply ideas practically
- Someone who is kind and friendly
- Making new friends
- Travel in connection with friends
- Original ideas
- Inventive and idealistic
- A new relationship
- Opportunities
- Good communication
- Poetry
- Adventure
- Mystery
- True love

NEGATIVE ASPECTS

- A person who is not as pleasant as they seem
- Someone who is not very truthful
- Unforeseen problems in a situation that seemed favourable
- Someone is deceived
- Unrequited love
- Someone who is afraid of telling the truth
- False hopes
- Someone who cant face up to some unpleasant truths
- Laziness
- Betrayal
- Bad news
- Victimization
- Selfishness
- Hypocritical
- Exaggeration
- A heartbreaker
- One night stand
- A trouble maker
- Obsession
- Over sensitive
- Emotional abuse
- Jumping to conclusions
- A heartbreaker

QUEEN OF CUPS

CARD OF BEAUTY

POSITIVE ASPECTS

- A dreamy looking woman
- Someone who day dreams
- Intuitive
- Sensitive
- A good wife and mother
- Acts with love
- Relies on intuition rather than reason
- Awaited pleasures and success are now coming
- Someone who is quiet and gentle
- Creative
- Kind and sympathetic
- Feminine
- Loyal
- Loving
- Shy
- Affectionate
- Maturity
- A family woman
- Deep thinker
- Great listener
- Good friend
- Friendly/Warm hearted
- An excellent advisor
- Intelligent and well educated
- A counsellor

NEGATIVE ASPECTS

- Someone who cannot be trusted
- Emotional immaturity
- Insecurity
- Lack of trust
- Lacking direction
- Weak
- Giving too much
- Overly-sensitive
- Needy
- Shallow
- Frivolous
- Blocked intuition
- Self-centered
- Disorganized
- Depressed
- Sulky
- Smothering
- Bitter
- Vengeful
- Manipulative
- Spiteful
- Unfaithful
- Self-centered
- Spiteful

KING OF CUPS

CARD OF A ROMANTIC

POSITIVE ASPECTS

- A magnetic, sexy man
- A man who keeps his emotions under control
- A very affectionate, very fair man
- Works in creative jobs or industries
- A very romantic man
- Honest
- A counsellor
- An excellent advisor
- A very strong person
- Trustworthy
- Very confident
- A man with lots of empathy
- In the field of arts and science
- A publisher
- A musician
- An artist
- A teacher
- Theatre plays
- A quiet man
- May makes decisions using intuition rather than reason
- Deep thinker
- A good friend
- Friendly/Warm hearted
- Great listener
- Intelligent and well educated

NEGATIVE ASPECTS

- Someone who can not be trusted
- An emotionally immature male
- Someone who takes advantage of others
- Emotional imbalance
- Manipulation
- A scam
- Hidden secrets
- Uncaring
- Gullible
- Depressed
- Dishonesty
- Controlling
- A conman
- Repressed
- Withdrawn
- Lazy
- Jealous
- Emotionally immature
- Overly emotional
- A cheater
- An affair
- Unbalanced
- Moody
- Anxious

SWORDS

ELEMENT: Air
STAR SIGNS: Aquarius, Libra and Gemini.
SEASON: Autumn
UNITS OF TIME: Hours or Days
ACE OF SWORDS: Approximately 1 Day

BRIEF DESCRIPTIONS:

Swords represent: the conscious and subconscious, powerful thoughts, mentality, worries, argument's, violence, actions that can be both constructive and destructive, hatred, enemies, battles, attitudes, negativity, belief's, double edged swords, anger, verbal and mental abuse, lack of compassion, guilty conscious, harsh judgments, medical, the law and death.

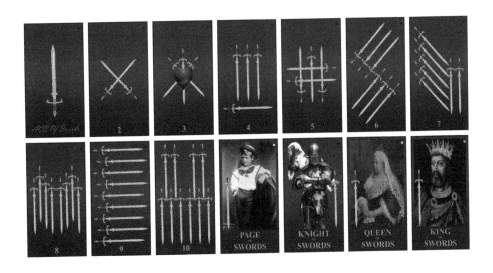

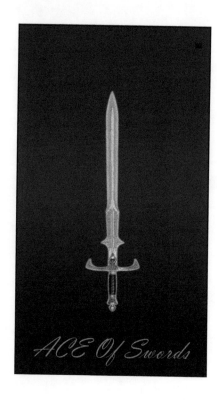

ACE OF SWORDS

CARD OF THOUGHT

POSITIVE ASPECTS

- Beginning of mental powers being used correctly
- Fresh ways of thinking
- Birth/New beginning
- Triumph in love or hatred
- Growth
- Victory
- Conception of a new idea
- Logical thinking
- Success and triumph
- Planning ahead
- Legal matters and or court case
- Taxation
- Power placed in your hands
- Surgery
- Medical investigations
- Injections
- Communications
- Speaking truth
- Cutting through problems
- Intellect
- Reason
- Justice
- Assertiveness
- Things moving quickly
- Strong visions

NEGATIVE ASPECTS

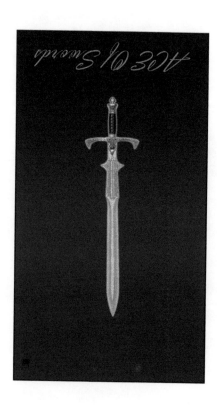

- Injustice
- Cruelty
- Misuse of power
- Clashes with authority
- Legal problems
- In a powerless position
- Unfavourable position in legal matters
- Painful treatment
- A cut or accident
- A lack of ideas
- Miscommunication
- Creative blocks
- Failure
- Hostility
- Memory loss
- Making the wrong decision/s
- Inability to focus
- Bad decisions
- Boredom
- Conflicts
- Defeat
- Misinformation
- Stress
- Negativity

2 OF SWORDS

CARD OF INDECISION

POSITIVE ASPECTS

- Law suit, justice will be done
- Using your mind and leaving emotions out of it
- Making a decision
- Can choose a direction
- Peace restored
- Can now see logically
- An agreement or settlement of some kind
- Truce
- Balance
- Maintaining peace at present by extreme caution
- Playing the roll of a peacemaker
- Allies
- Equally matched
- A worthy foe
- Sitting on the fence
- At the cross roads
- Facing your fears
- Caught in the middle
- A draw
- Conflict resolution
- Movement
- Action
- Decisions made with partial facts
- Stressful decisions
- Options

NEGATIVE ASPECTS

- Come to a standstill
- Not sure which way to go
- Subconscious, looking deeper
- Unrest in the emotions
- Closing of the heart
- Ready to strike anyone who comes too close
- In fear of losing balance
- Balance could be lost
- Psychical and emotional strain
- Finding peace at any price
- Always deciding between two things
- Stalemate in your affairs
- Needing a new approach
- Indication of being upset by a letter or a situation
- Unbalanced
- Delays
- Disagreements
- Conflicts
- Blindness
- Violence
- Hidden intentions
- Ruptures
- Insecurity
- Anxiety and stress

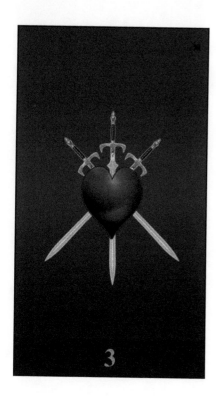

3 OF SWORDS

CARD OF HEARTACHE

POSITIVE ASPECTS

- Getting to the heart of the matter
- Healing from a broken heart
- Down in the dumps because of absence
- Distressing changes will make way for new and better experiences
- End of a time of loss and heartbreak
- The beginning of emotional and physical recovery
- Minor surgical procedures - (Possibly dental or other similar treatment)
- Overcoming depression
- Accepting growth from pain
- Short delay
- Letting go
- Lessons learnt
- Optimism
- Forgiveness
- Reconciliation
- Compromise
- Sharing problems
- Recovery
- Healing
- Blood test/s
- Improvement with blood pressure
- Improvement in heart health
- A blood transfusion

NEGATIVE ASPECTS

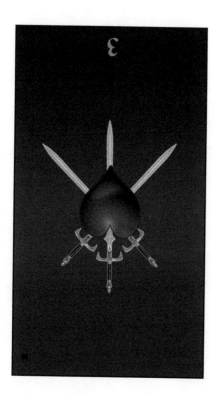

- Sorrow, heartbreak in any type of relationship
- Someone who is hurt
- Possible miscarriage due to misfortune
- Loved ones are separated
- Someone will be hurt if they find out
- Quarrelling caused a separation
- A current relationship is on rocky ground, maybe ending
- Upheaval in family situations upset and tears
- Illness and operations - (Especially to do with the heart and/or blood)
- Heart/Lung - (Waist up problems)
- Heart Attack
- Stroke
- Painful and difficult experiences
- Process of change is likely to be unpleasant
- Hostility and hurtful behavior
- Breakup, separation - (An ending of a relationship)
- Divorce
- Sorrow
- Strife
- Pain
- Death
- Funeral
- Depression

4 OF SWORDS

CARD OF REST AND RECOVERY

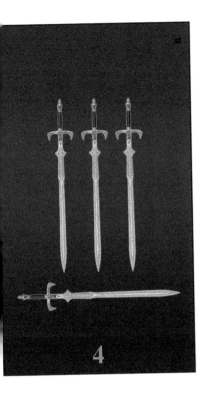

POSITIVE ASPECTS

- Self discipline
- Peace of mind
- In prayer or meditation, a blessing
- Planning for the future
- Ready for action
- Taking time out
- Vigilance
- Retreat
- Solitude
- Rest is required
- Recuperating
- Renewal of energy
- Give yourself time
- The situation is getting better
- Looking after yourself
- Retreat to a health farm
- Short stay in hospital
- Lesson period after illness
- Time off work
- A holiday
- Soul searching
- Hiding out
- Order
- Analysis
- Resting

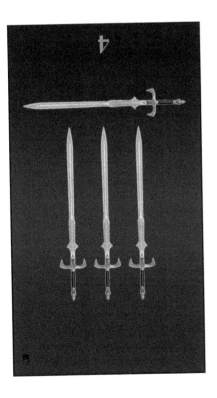

NEGATIVE ASPECTS

- Possible illness after accident
- Feeling of being cut off and out of touch
- Banishment
- Rejection
- Loneliness
- Death
- Grief
- Antisocialism
- Delay
- Stagnation
- Withdrawal
- Imprisonment
- Isolation
- Disorder
- Confinement
- Psychical exhaustion
- Mentally vulnerable
- Stress and anxiety
- Burn out
- Unrest
- Fear
- Contemplation
- Lack of ambition
- Depression

5 OF SWORDS

CARD OF ARGUMENTS AND DISAGREEMENTS

POSITIVE ASPECTS

- The Victor is all on his own
- Winning at all costs
- A minor victory
- Ruthlessness
- Standing up for what you believe in
- Knowing when to fight and when to retreat
- Peaceful resolution
- Ending of conflict
- Moving on
- Compromising
- Surrendering
- Relentless
- Taking a risk
- Making a sacrifice
- Improving communications
- Holding yourself accountable
- Cutting losses
- Reconciliation
- Resolution
- Revenge
- Forgiveness
- Unexpected change
- Fighting back
- Mind battles
- Setting rules

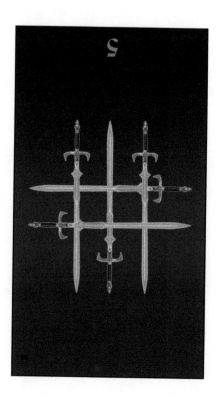

NEGATIVE ASPECTS

- Person could be very lonely
- Someone with an attitude problem
- A break up
- Severing of ties
- Someone has left abruptly
- Relationship has jus fallen apart
- Troublemaker or striker
- Battle of words gone too far
- Fighting a losing battle
- No reconciliation
- May indicate funerals
- Unfair dealings
- Ruined plans
- Hostility
- Lies
- Gossip
- Failure
- Loss
- Dejected
- Violence
- Jealousy
- Bullying
- Deception
- Dishonesty

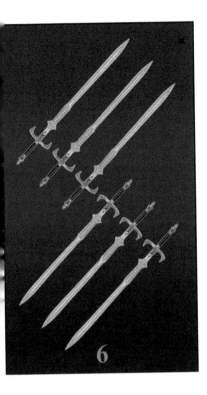

6 OF SWORDS

CARD OF MOVING AWAY FROM TROUBLE

POSITIVE ASPECTS

- Out of Rough water going into calm
- Moving into better times
- Moving away from troubles
- New life - (Any area of life)
- Peace after a journey
- Very deep thinking
- Been through difficult times
- A break needed
- Long journey
- Short holiday
- Overseas travel
- Overseas visitor coming
- Metaphorical move away from troubles
- On a mission
- Destination surrounded by lots of water - (An island)
- Making progress
- Relief
- Stability
- Overcoming hardship
- Guidance
- Support
- Balance
- Escaping
- Harmony
- A rescue

NEGATIVE ASPECTS

- Long and slow process of getting over a situation
- Unpleasant or frustrating work situations
- Severance of a relationship
- Troubling coming in
- Lack of progress
- Trapped
- Delays
- Rocking the boat
- Cancelled travel plans
- Floods
- Drowning
- Instability
- Troubled relationships
- Stuck
- Accident/s in the water
- Carrying baggage
- Unresolved plans
- The lack of courage and willpower
- Unknown destination
- Running away
- Refusing to deal with something emotionally
- Letting your fears take over you
- Seeing the worst in someone
- Shutting down your emotions

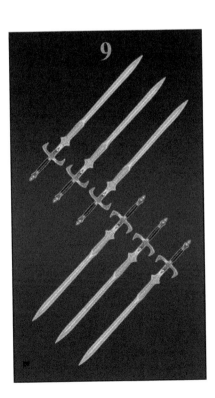

7 OF SWORDS

CARD OF DECEPTION

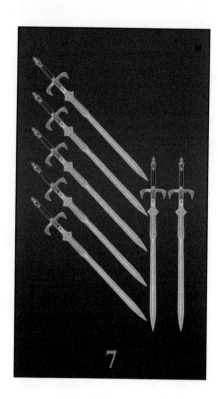

POSITIVE ASPECTS

- Move onwards, leaving the past behind
- Legal or insurance advice
- Forestalling trouble
- Avoiding direct confrontation
- Taking precautions
- Disarming your opposition
- Foresight
- Evasion
- Taking what's yours but your looking over your shoulder
- Confessing
- Turning over a new leaf
- Daring
- Carefully sneaking away
- Cunning
- Spying on your enemies
- Getting away with anything or everything
- Strategy - strategically planning
- Getting what you want
- All or nothing attitude
- Knowing when to take
- Trusting your instincts
- Keeping secrets from others
- Taking what you can
- Bargaining
- Coming back for more

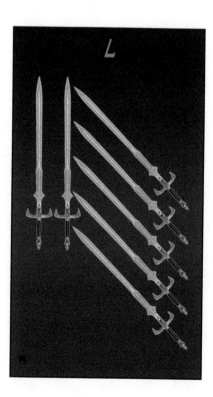

NEGATIVE ASPECTS

- Caution
- Instability, but not permanent
- Someone sneaking away - Helping themselves
- Taking advantage of you
- Acting alone
- Unwilling to get anyone's help
- One thing after another
- Theft
- Stealing ideas
- Hiding their intentions
- Does not want anyone to know what they are doing
- Someone undermining/putting something over on others
- Robbery
- Getting ripped off
- Avoiding communications
- Conservative behavior
- Frauds and scams
- Con artist
- Coward
- Two faced
- Pathological liar
- Cheater
- Treason
- Deception

8 OF SWORDS

CARD OF RESTRICTION

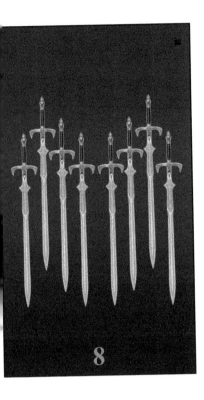

POSITIVE ASPECTS

- A run of bad luck will pass soon
- Temporary restrictions
- Self-imprisonment
- The situation may not be as difficult as it seems
- Slight progress
- Escape
- Freedom
- A period of relief
- Taking control
- Healing
- Finding strength
- Finding solutions and options
- Facing your fears
- An end to punishment
- Released from prison
- Empowered
- A healthier mental state
- New perspective
- Hopeful
- Releasing anxiety
- A survivor
- Liberation
- Open to new perspectives
- Weight loss
- Healing

NEGATIVE ASPECTS

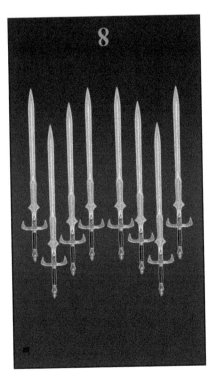

- Restrictions
- Isolation from other people
- Feeling alone with no help
- Confusion
- Oppressive ideas
- Bad news
- Conflict
- Sickness
- Tied into a situation that is out of your hands
- Worry acting as an energy block
- Multitude of problems
- Mental stress
- Anxiety
- Hard times surround you
- Possible trouble with the law
- Disappointments
- Accidents
- Locked up - (Possibly jail)
- Someone who has problems with their eyes
- Headaches/migraines
- Upper body problems - (Tight chest)
- Abuse
- Letting people control you
- Playing the victim

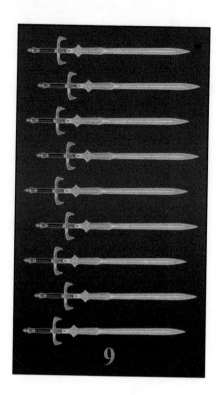

9 OF SWORDS

CARD OF WORRY AND SLEEPLESS NIGHTS

POSITIVE ASPECTS

- Worrying for nothing
- Time and courage will heal the wounds
- Recovering
- Letting go of negativity
- Overcoming anxiety
- Better nights sleep
- Letting go of stress
- Improved health
- Accepting help
- Learning to cope
- Optimism
- Gaining clarity
- The worst is now passed
- A nightshift worker
- It was just all in your head
- A renewal of hope
- Ready to face reality
- Overcoming your fears
- A new bed
- Overthinking
- Overcoming of night terrors
- Letting it all out
- Overcoming of negative thoughts
- A mother who worries about her children
- Overcoming depression

NEGATIVE ASPECTS

- Loss
- Anxiety
- Oppression
- Despair
- Misery
- Grief
- Failure
- Loss
- Disappointment
- Sadness
- Sleepless nights
- Serious illness
- Miscarriage
- Nightmares
- Hopelessness
- Health problems
- Headaches / migraines
- Loneliness
- Crying
- Depression
- A breakdown
- Regret
- A feeling of extreme guilt
- Negative thoughts

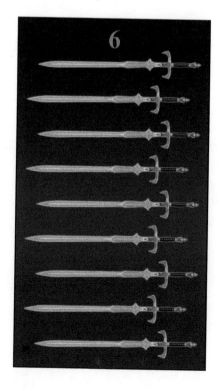

10 OF SWORDS

CARD OF BETRAYAL

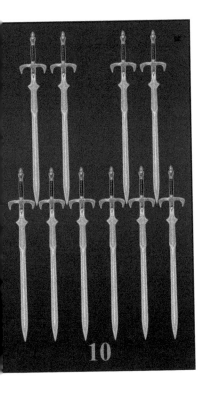

POSITIVE ASPECTS

- An ending to a painful situation
- The beginning of a new phase
- Learning from the past
- Rebuilding
- Survival
- Improvement
- Healing
- Fighting back
- Recovery
- Regeneration
- New ways cope
- Forgiveness
- Successful back surgery
- The worst is now over
- Going back to something
- Someone is coming back
- Cant get any worse
- Acupuncture
- Catching the gossiper
- Strengthening ones back
- An end to all mental pain and fatigue
- Back to basics
- Triumph over evil
- Better days are coming
- A change for the better

NEGATIVE ASPECTS

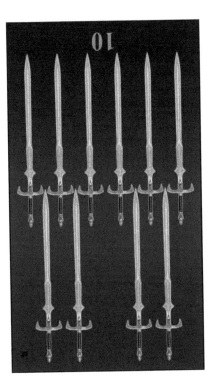

- A feeling of being stabbed in the back
- Someone with back trouble or back ache
- Pain inflicted
- Tears
- Sadness
- Feeling ill
- A betrayal of confidence and trust
- Someone going behind your back
- An ending in any area
- Extreme unhappiness
- Depression
- Deep sense of loss
- Legal situation
- Social distress
- Unfortunate collapse of plans which is difficult to accept
- Separation
- Treachery
- A forced change
- Health matters - injections and medical investigations
- Crisis
- Betrayal
- Failure
- Dead end
- Playing victim

PAGE OF SWORDS

CARD OF ANARCHY

POSITIVE ASPECTS

- A sporty child
- Beginning of legal, medical or other professional help
- A child who is clever and serious
- The ability to complete what has been started
- A document or contract of importance
- Somebody starting out again - (In studies)
- Determination
- Awakening mind
- The ability to succeed
- Mental alert
- Someone who stands up for what they believe in
- Sharpening of mental faculties
- Someone who is looking out for you
- A very quick phone call
- Someone with lots of questions to ask
- Remote viewing / online conversations
- Supervision
- Exams
- Talking their way out of conflict
- Always knows their surroundings
- Quick witted
- Being truthful
- Fighting injustice
- Curious
- Energetic energy

NEGATIVE ASPECTS

- Somebody who cant see the point
- Defensive or aggressive
- Check things out before signing and agreeing
- Activities could be causing some concern
- Possible delay in plans
- News you will consider disappointing
- A hypocritical person
- An interrogation
- Bad news
- A spy
- Someone who spends too much time watching and judging others
- Malicious gossip
- Mind games
- Lacking ideas
- Head in the clouds
- Cold hearted
- Someone with learning difficulties
- Arguments
- Immaturity
- Lack of education
- Not speaking out
- A player
- Scatterbrain

KNIGHT OF SWORDS

CARD OF AGILITY

POSITIVE ASPECTS

- Moving quickly
- Quick thinking
- New ideas
- Full charge ahead
- Impulsive
- Confident
- Quick mental ability (always on the go)
- Ready to attack
- A young man with good intentions
- Sudden change
- Letters
- Phone calls
- Information arriving suddenly
- An old friend or lover could suddenly appear
- Ready for a challenge
- Pushing harder
- A clever, intellectual and ambitious young man
- Someone who favours you and will defend you
- An aggressive approach
- Self-assured
- Courageous and in action
- Driven to succeed
- Ambitious
- Assertive
- Action orientated

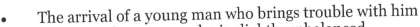

NEGATIVE ASPECTS

- The arrival of a young man who brings trouble with him
- An aggressive person who is slightly unbalanced
- Someone with an overbearing attitude
- A bully
- Destruction
- Conflict
- Physically aggressive (uses their hands)
- Someone who doesn't think before they speak
- Uses words that cut deep
- Spiteful arguments
- Restless
- Unfocused
- Arrogance
- A clever liar
- Deceitful
- Being out of control
- Making reckless mistakes
- Lack of patience
- Constantly changing mind and direction
- Scattered energies
- A coward
- Bad advice
- Heartless
- Missed opportunities

QUEEN OF SWORDS

CARD OF INTEGRITY

Positive Aspects

- A clever logical quick witted woman
- Someone who is widowed or divorced
- Occupations in the field of law and medical or anyone who wears a uniform or suit
- Someone who is cool and charming
- Heart is ruled by a cool head
- Someone who gives help and reliable advice
- Very strong and clear headed in a crisis
- Someone who is an excellent dancer and fond of music
- A good counsellor
- Someone who well disciplined and in control of themselves
- Independent
- Honest
- Truthful
- Someone who is a strong, balanced thinker
- Intelligent
- Protective
- Someone who loves the social life
- Witty
- Principled
- Great advice
- Someone who is very idealistic
- Open minded
- Quirky
- Someone in command of authority

Negative Aspects

- Rude
- A lack of empathy
- Pessimistic
- Malicious
- Bitter
- Manipulative
- Poor communicator
- Repressed trauma
- Pessimistic
- Aggressive
- Bitter
- Bad tempered
- A cheater
- Likes to hurt others
- Cruel
- Unrelaxed
- Gossiper
- Revengeful
- Heartless
- Unforgiving
- Repeats mistakes
- Excessive negativity
- Skeptical
- Cold and blunt

KING OF SWORDS

CARD OF INTELLECT

POSITIVE ASPECTS

- A clever, logical, quick-witted man
- Someone who is widowed or divorced
- Occupations in the field of law and medical
- Someone with authority, or who wears a uniform or suit
- Someone who gives helpful and reliable advice
- Honest and truthful
- Someone who thinks before committing themselves
- Self-discipline
- Someone who is very cautious
- Adaptable and a peace maker
- A diplomat
- Someone who is ready for action
- Gift of the gab
- Bit of a flirt
- Someone with excellent judgment
- Logical
- Someone who is really good with puzzles, chess and card games
- Someone with lots of mental activity
- Analytical
- Ethical
- Integrity
- Morals
- Uses their head over their heart

NEGATIVE ASPECTS

- Someone who is a sarcastic, aggressive person
- A dangerous person who's company is best avoided
- Takes advantage of their power
- Someone who thinks they are above others
- Illogical
- A lack of integrity
- Irrational
- Power crazed
- Someone who uses his power to manipulate or bully
- A dictator
- Oppressive
- Inhumane
- Aggressive
- Brutal
- Someone who is extremely unkind and cruel
- Violent
- Intimidating
- Controlling
- Someone who is hard to live with
- Cold hearted
- Stubborn
- Someone with a sharp tongue
- Lack of intelligence
- Someone who has a big head

PENTACLES

ELEMENT: Earth
STAR SIGNS: Taurus, Virgo and Capricorn
SEASON: Winter
UNITS OF TIME: Years
ACE OF SWORDS: Approximately 1 Year

BRIEF DESCRIPTIONS:

Pentacles represent: materialistic aspects of life including work, business, property, trade, prosperity, proof, realization, manifestation, financial matters, and finances. Investments, borrowing, planning, country and warm locations

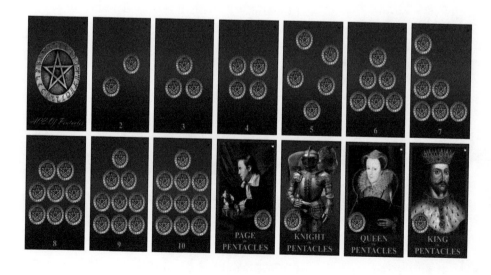

ACE OF PENTACLES

CARD OF SETTING GOALS

POSITIVE ASPECTS

- Job offering
- A goal in sight but a long way in the distance
- Plans of starting a business
- Beginning of a creation
- Successful venture
- Successful plans
- Prosperity
- In a position to spend big
- A new and better paid job
- Entering a productive phase
- A job that requires using your hands
- Being careful with your money
- Significant improvement with your finances
- Abundance
- Wealth
- Good fortune
- A windfall
- Raise in salary
- A large payment is on the way
- An educational degree
- Strong foundations
- Garden growth
- Maintenance of a garden
- New ideas
- Investments

NEGATIVE ASPECTS

- Gambling
- Lack of money
- Poor financial control
- Lost or a lack of opportunities
- Delays in financial matters
- Excessive spending
- Scarcity
- Deficiency
- Poor planning
- Instability
- Insecurity
- Cancellations
- Greed
- Stinginess
- Hard work is needed
- A small amount of money
- Failures
- Dishonest earnings
- Penny pinching
- Bad investments
- Loss of money or job
- Bad financial decisions
- Invested in the wrong career
- Money issues in a relationship

2 OF PENTACLES

CARD OF JUGGLING

POSITIVE ASPECTS

- Financial balance
- Fluctuating fortunes
- Desire for balance and continuance of activity
- Balancing a budget
- Desire for lasting quality
- Someone who is self-employed with uncertain income
- Making a decision on which way to go
- Coping with 2 situations
- Someone with strong legs
- Strong characteristics
- Stamina
- Able to cope and manage
- Expect to receive acknowledgment
- Reassuring news
- A small sum of money
- More ups than downs
- Adaptability
- Harmonious change
- Adaptability
- Balancing books
- Transferring money
- Profit
- Partnership
- Confidence
- A letter

NEGATIVE ASPECTS

- Juggling with money - borrowing from Peter to pay Paul
- Breakup of a partnership
- Subsequent splitting of resources
- Need for awareness and observation
- Fluctuation
- Stillness
- Lack of resources
- Trouble
- Embarrassment
- Lack of money
- Loss of balance
- Poor financial decisions
- Overwhelmed
- Overextended
- Financial loss
- No contingency plan
- Physical weakness
- Lack of confidence
- Instability
- Vanity
- More downs than ups
- Unable to adapt
- Lack of organization

3 OF PENTACLES

CARD OF ENQUIRY

POSITIVE ASPECTS

- Success through skill
- Successful project
- Everything is going according to plan
- Progression in skills
- Enquiring about a job
- A paid job
- Working hard to master a craft
- Efforts will be rewarded
- Home improvements - inside or out
- Someone starting their own business
- Change in job
- Someone with great skill, ability and talent
- Recognition or award
- Move of house
- An opportunity to earn money
- New learnings
- Studying
- Growth
- Commitment
- Goals
- Collaboration
- Dedication
- Attention to detail
- An apprenticeship
- A higher skill level

NEGATIVE ASPECTS

- Not learning from mistakes
- Lack of growth
- Unwillingness to learn
- Lack of effort
- Mistakes
- Lack of work
- Apathy
- Lack of determination
- No goal setting
- Lack of motivation
- Work done with poor quality
- Disharmony
- Lack of commitment
- Misalignment
- Lack of knowledge
- Someone who is the subject of envy
- Unskilled labor
- Poor work ethic
- Small wages
- Loss of a job
- Financial problems
- Lack of direction
- Inexperience
- Lack of respect

4 OF PENTACLES

CARD OF SECURITY

POSITIVE ASPECTS

- Financial security
- Hanging on to what you have
- There will soon be money in the bank
- Protecting themselves
- Not wealth but continual comfort
- Someone who is not fussy about their appearance
- Past materials and accomplishments
- Dealing with the material side of life
- Well balanced
- An increase in power and responsibility
- Fond of being in charge
- Someone who likes power
- Strongly attached to materialistic pursuits and endeavours
- Possible receipt of a gift
- Stability
- Someone who works very hard for money
- Holding on to your possessions
- Deep seated
- Saving
- Generosity
- Sharing
- Making large purchases
- Self protection
- Investments
- Possible inheritance

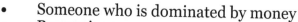

NEGATIVE ASPECTS

- Someone who is dominated by money
- Possessiveness
- Someone who needs to balance out their money
- Insecurity
- Greed
- Someone who needs psychic protection
- Financial loss
- Gambling
- A Hoarder
- Possessiveness
- Someone who likes to control
- Scarcity
- Delays
- Someone who doesn't have much money
- Anxious
- Uncertainty
- Fear of loss
- Someone who needs to watch their money
- Jealousy
- Holding on to the past
- A clingy lover
- Paranoia
- Avoiding collaboration

5 OF PENTACLES

CARD OF HARDSHIP

POSITIVE ASPECTS

- Love is holding people together in a bad situation
- Light and love is there if you look around
- Battles are a time for learning
- Change of direction to find more in life
- Help is on the way
- Temporary financial hardship
- Improvement in finances
- End of hardship
- Positive change
- Becoming financially secure
- Overcoming adversity
- Paying off debts
- Coming out of debt
- Finding employment
- An amazing love life
- Good partnerships
- Loyal friends
- Fulfilling sex life
- Happy heart
- Stable housing
- Taking things one step at a time
- Overcoming grief and loss
- Forgiveness
- Acceptance
- Overcoming isolation and loneliness

NEGATIVE ASPECTS

- Loss of faith
- Poverty
- Material Trouble
- People becoming destitute
- Hardship
- Church or religion has failed to give comfort so have moved on
- Unemployment
- Ill health
- A breakup
- Self-worth is the enemy
- Financial loss
- Feeling neglected
- Emotional support in the wrong place
- Love affairs will go well but will be short term
- Negative change
- Adversity
- Struggle
- Homelessness
- Poverty
- Divorce
- Disgrace
- Bankruptcy
- Scandal

6 OF PENTACLES

CARD OF GIVING AND RECEIVING

POSITIVE ASPECTS

- Showing generosity
- A giver
- Presents
- Gifts
- Prosperity
- Generosity
- Charity
- Legacy
- A bonus
- Good things are happening
- You will receive what's rightfully yours
- What you give out comes back in - karma
- Ask and you shell receive
- Practical help from a person
- Receiving a certain amount
- You'll soon be in a position to spend money
- In a position to pay off any debts
- A share out
- Favours can now be repaid
- Promotion
- Investors
- Equality
- Power
- Authority
- Profit

NEGATIVE ASPECTS

- Theft
- Being cheated
- Used
- Abusing generosity
- Gift with strings attached
- Subservience
- Inequality
- Lack of charity
- Abuse of power
- Scams
- Lack of investments
- Undervalued
- Bad debts
- Stealing
- Sucking up to someone
- No help from anyone
- Disloyalty
- Disdain
- Extravagance
- Extortion
- Power dynamics
- Hidden agendas
- Resentment
- No financial support

7 OF PENTACLES

CARD OF HARD WORK

POSITIVE ASPECTS

- Early growth and gradually growing
- Slow growth
- Long term advancement
- Thing will come to fruition eventually
- Seeing results
- Planning your next move during this phase of activity
- Period of hard work paying off
- Productive work on a non material basis
- In the process of making a major decision
- Welcome change in your financial situation
- Rewards
- Results
- Manifestation of ideas or goals
- Perseverance
- Gestation
- Cultivation
- Retirement
- Commitment
- Stability
- Determined
- Reviewing
- Change of direction
- A Payout
- Recovery
- Investment decisions

NEGATIVE ASPECTS

- Not enough effort being made
- No rewards for resting
- Anxious in the process of negotiating money
- Much work with little gain
- Concern about repayments of a loan
- Working for something where you're not getting paid
- Bad business management
- Poor financial management
- Not finishing what you started
- Laziness
- Lack of growth
- Setbacks
- Delays
- Impatience
- Lack of vision
- Debts
- Restriction
- Resignation
- Uncertainty
- Failed investment
- Unemployment
- Wasted energy
- Procrastination
- Impatience

8 OF PENTACLES

CARD OF SKILLS AND DEVELPOMENT

POSITIVE ASPECTS

- New skills
- Employment
- Courses
- A trade
- Can earn money through skills
- An artist
- New orders for business
- Persist and you will learn
- Training
- Training that brings discipline and skill
- Careful financial management
- Small savings
- Patience
- Attention to detail
- Crafting a known skill set
- Steady work
- Stability
- Preparing for the future
- Studying
- Dedicated to a personal goal
- New job
- Promotion
- Qualifications
- Concentration
- Expertise

NEGATIVE ASPECTS

- Boring job
- Failure
- Lack of concentration
- Poor focus
- Lack of ambition
- Poor quality
- Bad reputation
- Mediocrity
- Financial insecurity
- Under qualified
- Poor skills
- Workaholic
- Impatience
- Delays
- Dead end career
- Not seeing results
- Ambition collapse
- Problems at work or with a job
- Misdirected activity
- Greed
- Criticism
- Treachery
- Low salary
- Overspending

9 OF PENTACLES

CARD OF GROWTH

POSITIVE ASPECTS

- Material well-being
- Safety
- Success
- Pleasure and gain
- Someone who is well off
- Love of home and garden
- Gardening
- Someone who has a career or hobby in gardening
- Hard work has paid off
- Someone who is always well dressed
- Financial security
- In a position to buy and sell
- Buy new clothes and or furniture
- Completion of the season - ready to 'harvest'
- Love of nature
- Outdoor activities
- Money and success are on the way
- Improvements with land and property
- Someone who is very knowledgeable and handles their affairs very well
- Independence
- A profit
- Wealth
- A thriving business
- Freedom

NEGATIVE ASPECTS

- Still seeking a purpose in life
- Need for security
- Incompletion
- Someone who thinks they have it all but they don't
- Dependency
- Still seeking inner satisfaction
- Financial dependency
- Someone who is marrying for money
- Prostitution
- Deceit
- Theft
- Superficial
- Lack of style
- Financial setbacks
- Lack of elegance
- Bad investments
- Loss of money
- Problems with property
- Fraud
- Addictions
- Losses
- Deprivation
- Impulse purchases
- A female with reproductive issues

10 OF PENTACLES

CARD OF ABUNDANCE

POSITIVE ASPECTS

- Buying, selling or renting out of property
- Financial gain
- Wise family observing the future
- Attainment comes from achieving balance
- Family matters
- Finances beginning to prosper
- Practical help from the family
- Material comfort
- Decisions in property
- Pleasure from achievement
- Success
- Financial security
- Happy family life
- Good friends surround you
- Receiving a pension
- A rise in salary
- Travel in connection to business
- Starting a business
- Recognition
- Family business
- Stability
- Legacy
- Tradition
- An inheritance
- Attaining whatever you think of as success

NEGATIVE ASPECTS

- Family disputes
- Bankruptcy
- Debt/s
- Conflict over money
- Instability
- Family member with a negative influence on you
- Breaking traditions
- Unstable career
- Failure in business
- Financial loss
- Conflict between love and family
- Restrictive culture
- Theft
- Unsuccessful
- Lack of motivation
- Confiscation
- Family parting
- Gambling addictions
- Lack of stability
- Disloyalty
- Divorce
- Fake wealth
- Unconventional
- Lack of resources

PAGE OF PENTACLES

CARD OF STUDIES

POSITIVE ASPECTS

- News about money
- Minor rise in salary or income
- Something new, afresh
- New growth
- Someone in an apprenticeship - farming, horticulture
- A meeting with someone kind and generous
- Someone who is very tidy and particular about their appearance
- Someone who is into fashion and clothing
- A hairdresser
- Someone who is imaginative and looks into the future
- A young person who enjoys studying and is a persevering scholar
- An older, introverted child who prefers books and quiet games
- Someone who gives you good news that will change many things
- Changes for the better
- Someone with a good natured personality
- A meeting with someone who is kind, generous and sympathetic to your views
- Setting goals
- Developing a plan
- Laying foundations
- Excellent prospects

NEGATIVE ASPECTS

- Unexpected bills
- A warning against theft
- Concerns about choices that are made
- Lack of goals
- Lacking common sense
- Lazy
- Foolish
- Immature
- No groundwork
- An underachiever
- Not seeing opportunities
- Dark magic
- Lack of progress
- Procrastination
- No follow through
- Unrealistic plans
- Lack of motivation
- Trouble within school or education
- Failed studies
- Unable to budget
- Missed business opportunities
- Not wanting to work for money
- Short term career
- Lack of confidence

KNIGHT OF PENTACLES
CARD OF SLOW MOVEMENT

POSITIVE ASPECTS

- Trustworthy person
- Ambition and determination
- Loyal friend or a business partner
- Someone who is sensible, practical and dependable
- Boring job that does achieve something
- An improvement in finances
- Good worker who plods along
- Someone with a very earthly mind
- Working in the gardens
- Young man who is thorough and will take time to do a good job
- Someone who will not experiment outside their goal
- Love for animals and nature
- Someone who is good with money on the development of land and its products
- Travel or movement in connection with money and business
- A veterinarian
- Studies
- Patient
- Practical
- Responsible
- Persistence
- Reliable
- Stability
- Protection

NEGATIVE ASPECTS

- Slow, not getting anywhere
- Someone who can lack imagination
- Dull job
- Tardiness
- Stubbornness
- Someone who needs consistent motivation
- Possessiveness
- Jealousy
- Delays
- Calculus
- Unstable
- Disloyal
- Irresponsible
- Weak
- A gambler
- Broken promises
- Not finishing what you start
- Boring
- Impatient
- Lack of empathy
- Workaholic
- Risky investments
- Neglecting a relationship
- Impulsive purchases

QUEEN OF PENTACLES

CARD OF PROPERTY AND LAND

POSITIVE ASPECTS

- A very fertile and fruitful, warm hearted lady
- Woman who is into arts, crafts, knitting, embroidery, tapestry
- Achieving material success
- Desire for security and success
- Someone who enjoys good food, clothes and nice places
- Successful business woman
- Someone who is interested in history and old buildings
- Someone who is at peace
- A creative woman with many talents
- Someone with many talents
- A steady, clever business woman
- Someone is family orientated and charitable
- Woman who is practical, capable, reliable and conscientious
- Someone who fights hard for their rights in any dispute
- Wealth
- Someone who is very organized
- Luxurious
- Practical
- A love for the country
- Wonderful mother
- Fertility
- Vitality
- Realistic

NEGATIVE ASPECTS

- Lady who requires a stable financial partner
- Someone who needs their own space
- Ungrounded
- Someone who can be withdrawn
- Jealous
- Mean
- Cheater
- Possessive
- Out of control
- Weight issues
- A prostitute
- Disorganized
- Manipulator
- Dark magic
- Bad mother
- Cunning
- Moneygrubbing
- Poor reputation
- Gold digger
- Materialistically obsessed
- Envious of others success
- Unreliable
- Unskilled
- Poor financial management

KING OF PENTACLES

CARD OF FINANCE AND INVESTMENT

POSITIVE ASPECTS

- Successful business man who has achieved what he wants in life
- Financially secure
- A very gifted man who is highly intelligent
- Someone who is close to nature
- Very loyal and reliable man in relationships
- Loyal and steadfast
- Large companies or well established organizations
- Someone who works in banking, investments
- Someone who works in real estate
- A competent man in mathematical procedures
- Someone who is generous, friendly and affectionate
- A practical approach to resources and a successful outcome to business matters
- Someone who gives great advice and help
- A provider
- Dependable
- Conservative
- Stability
- Wealthy
- An empire
- Cooperation
- Practicality
- Prosperity

NEGATIVE ASPECTS

- Someone who is too materialistic
- Ungrounded
- An unsuccessful business man
- Corruption in business matter
- Someone who is a dull companion
- Extortion
- Instability
- Broke
- Gambler
- Bankruptcy
- Greedy
- Hasty
- Unfaithful
- Cold
- Ruthless
- Obstinate
- Commercialism
- Fanaticism
- Insensitivity
- Obsession
- A dishonest act
- Illegal activities
- A workaholic
- Risky investments and decisions

WANDS

ELEMENT: Fire
STAR SIGNS: Leo, Sagittarius and Aries.
SEASON: Spring
UNITS OF TIME: Months
ACE OF SWORDS: Approximately 1 Month

BRIEF DESCRIPTIONS:

Wands represent: fast moving, actions, high energies, inspiration, determination, strength, intuition, solutions, creativity, development, ambitions, courage, expansion, success, success in business, the launching of ideas, the never ending list of things to do, projects, busy, egos, enthusiasm and day to day duties.

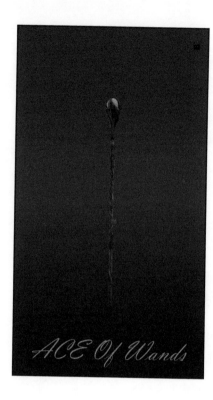

ACE OF WANDS

CARD OF TAKING ACTION

POSITIVE ASPECTS

- The beginning of starting something new
- A new way of life
- New interests or a creative hobby
- Power and growth
- Invention
- A birth
- Inspiration
- Birth of an idea
- In control of emotion
- Activities in social or business affairs
- Career opportunities
- Important message
- Accepting any invitations offered
- Enthusiasm
- Action
- Accepting a challenge
- Fun and excitement
- Talent
- Travel
- Good news
- Energy
- A breakthrough
- Will power
- Movement
- Creation

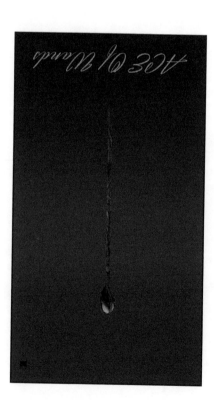

NEGATIVE ASPECTS

- Lack of focus
- Delays
- Bad news
- Creative blockages
- Lack of initiative
- Missed chances
- Cancelled travel plans
- Hesitation
- Wasted talent
- Lack of enthusiasm
- Problems with pregnancy
- Disappointments
- Lack of motivation
- Obstacles
- Distractions
- Burnt out
- Stagnation
- Lack of willpower
- Low self esteem
- All talk and no action
- Lacking goals and direction
- Cancelations
- Rejecting an offer
- Boredom

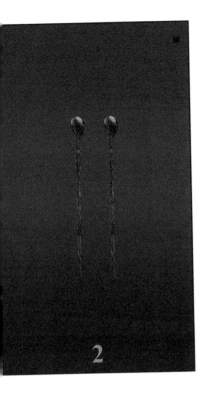

2 OF WANDS

CARD OF SURVEYANCE

POSITIVE ASPECTS

- Surveying a situation
- Looking out for something new
- Have done well in the past but still a lot more to do
- Property settlement
- Someone who is into bowling
- Looking into the future
- Someone with tremendous ability and foresight
- A business partnership
- Two paths
- Looking into new areas in business or property
- Options
- Opportunity
- Cooperation
- Suddenly leaving
- Waiting for the right thing
- Restlessness
- Anticipation
- Detachment
- Aiming high
- Visions
- High expectations
- Efficiency
- Planning
- Ambition
- In control

NEGATIVE ASPECTS

- Isolated
- Loneliness
- Someone who has their life together but is still too young to retire
- Fear of change
- Limited options
- Indecisiveness
- Lack of planning
- Fearing the unknown
- Delayed travel
- Cancellations
- Held back
- Doubts
- Discontent
- Communication gap
- Unfulfilled
- Grass isn't always greener
- Poor planning
- Stress
- Conflicts
- Losing control
- Stubbornness
- Sudden change
- Someone who is bored and needs new ideas

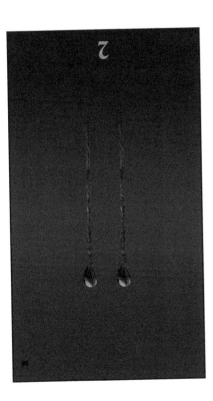

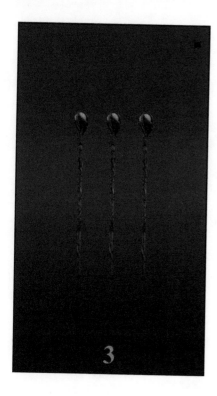

3 OF WANDS
CARD OF EXPECTANCY

POSITIVE ASPECTS

- A feeling of expectancy
- What's next
- Your ship is now coming in
- Letting go of the past
- Overseas interest
- Looking for new areas
- In command of themselves
- Business can prosper
- Someone who is well groomed
- Keeping a solid basis in business or commerce
- Someone who is willing to give assistance
- The right teammate could enhance a project and bring required success
- News and negotiations regarding business or work matters
- Travel
- Forward planning
- Self-belief
- Freedom
- Success
- Happy outcomes
- Hard work paying off
- Something in the distance you can see
- Luck is on your side
- Opportunities
- Leadership

NEGATIVE ASPECTS

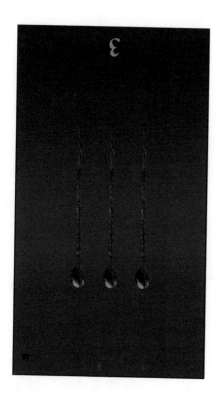

- Holding on to the past
- A lack of forward planning
- Self-doubt
- Lack of growth
- Failure
- Unhappy with choices
- A poor leader
- Plans that fall through
- Unhappy with outcomes
- Treachery
- Insecurities
- Obstacles
- Unrealistic plans
- Disappointment
- Negligence
- Lack of support
- An unreliable person
- Stagnation
- Lack of drive
- Restrictions
- Lack of growth
- Limitations
- Frustration
- Lack of progress

4 OF WANDS

CARD OF THE HOME

POSITIVE ASPECTS

- Work accomplished
- A time to celebrate
- Harmony
- Peace
- Family celebration
- Prosperity
- Buying or selling property
- A happy holiday
- A second home
- Freedom
- Someone who is involved in property
- Career in dancing, theatre and music
- Home renovations
- Working on property
- Creative enterprise will go well
- Coming home
- A wedding
- Success
- Prosperity
- A reunion
- Recognition
- Team work
- Self-esteem
- Proud of success
- A country house

NEGATIVE ASPECTS

- Unhappy families
- Cancelled reunion
- Self-doubt
- Lack of self esteem
- Cancelled celebrations
- Feeling unwelcome
- Ignorance
- A breakup
- Instability
- Lack of security
- Delays
- Disagreements
- Tensions
- Imbalanced
- Unwanted change
- Mistrust
- Lack of confidence
- Loss of power
- Change of the status quo
- Rejection
- Disharmony
- Unstable finances
- Workplace conflicts
- Burdens

5 OF WANDS

CARD OF COMPETITION AND CHALLENGES

POSITIVE ASPECTS

- Healthy competition
- Flirtation
- Competitiveness
- Testing of one's strength
- Working as a team
- Building
- You will accept a challenge which calls for patience and courage but you'll win through in the end
- Sharing ideas
- Sports and games
- A test
- An end to conflict
- Compromise
- An end to struggle
- Peace
- A solution
- Harmony
- You're liked by more than one person
- Avoiding conflict
- Sexual energy
- Ambition
- Self-confidence
- Passion
- Chance to show your skill
- Sportsmanship

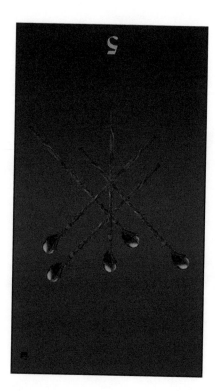

NEGATIVE ASPECTS

- Struggle in situations (matters)
- Not achieving anything
- Wasted energies
- Struggling in search after riches
- Everyone trying to do it their way
- Situation that flares up
- A need to consolidate ideas
- Conflict
- Fighting
- Struggling
- Arguing
- Disagreements
- Battles
- Tempers
- Egos clash
- Strikes
- Rough
- Chaos
- Extreme aggression
- Seeking conflict
- Fighting for ones attention
- Quarreling
- Tension
- Strife

6 OF WANDS

CARD OF VICTORY

POSITIVE ASPECTS

- Victory
- Promotion in regards to business
- Good news to be announced
- Success
- Recognition
- Achievement
- Faith and optimism
- Confidence
- Winning
- Pride
- Advantaged
- Praise
- Rewards
- Acclaim
- Fame
- Goodwill
- Supporters
- Crowds
- Being in the spotlight
- Strength
- A leader
- Progress
- Success in business
- A strong identity
- Triumph

NEGATIVE ASPECTS

- News which no one will agree with
- Not good news for everybody
- A waiting period
- Failure
- Lack of achievement
- Poor recognition
- Losing
- Lack of confidence
- Egotism
- Disadvantaged
- Being hunted
- Ill-will
- Fame hungry
- Disappointments
- Disgraced
- Pride before a fall
- Fall from grace
- Arrogance
- Snobbishness
- Disdain
- Highhandedness
- Over dominant
- Defeated
- Betrayal

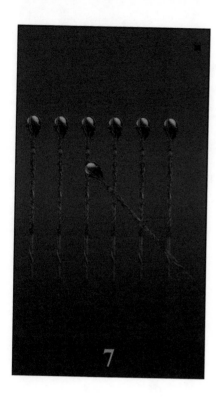

7 OF WANDS

CARD OF ATTACK

POSITIVE ASPECTS

- On the defense or attack
- Going to have a go
- Sticking to your guns
- Coming out on top
- Inner strength
- Seeing things more clearly
- Rest from undue tensions
- Determination
- Great force in attack
- Protective
- Strong will
- Challenging
- Stamina
- Territorial
- Courage
- Bravery
- Virtue
- Action
- Persistence
- Honesty
- Self-confidence
- Using physical strength
- Expansion
- Advantaged
- Perseverance

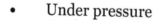

NEGATIVE ASPECTS

- Under pressure
- Battling to overcome life's problems
- Someone under pressure at work
- Be careful how you tred
- Be sure before you take steps
- Been provoked
- Giving up
- Admitting defeat
- Quitting
- Surrendering
- Weak
- Timid
- Lack of courage
- Failing to protect
- Overbearing
- Loss of control
- Burnt-out
- Blame
- Frustration
- Conflicts
- Stubbornness
- Vanity
- Setbacks
- Giving up on your beliefs

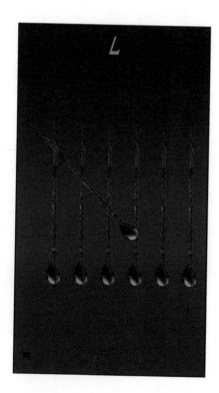

8 OF WANDS

CARD OF QUICK MOVEMENT

POSITIVE ASPECTS

- Things are on the move
- Air travel
- Journey
- Communications
- Connections with overseas travel
- Something coming in swiftly
- Good news coming from overseas
- Travel connected to business
- Business expansion
- New ideas
- Acceleration in your affairs - Any area of your life
- Something coming in fast
- Speed
- Action
- Learning
- An education or career in travel
- Progress
- Exciting times
- Freedom
- A holiday
- Results
- Solutions
- Jumping in
- Being swept off your feet
- Fast changes

NEGATIVE ASPECTS

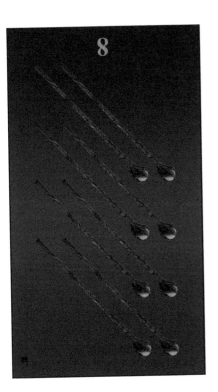

- A love affair
- Hastiness
- Lack of speed
- Slowness
- Bad news travels fast
- Delays
- Slow progress
- Out of control
- Bad timing
- Cancelled travel plans
- Restrictions
- Missed opportunity
- Impatience
- Impulsive
- Panic
- Lack of energy
- Insecurity
- Gossip
- Thoughtlessness
- Fluctuations
- Frustration
- Obstruction
- Unreliability
- Stagnation

9 OF WANDS

CARD OF ON GUARD

POSITIVE ASPECTS

- Ready to go again
- Recovery from illness
- Protecting own affairs
- Holding on to what you believe
- Ready for battle
- On firm ground
- Guarded
- Pushing forward
- Persistence
- Learning from the past
- Gathering strength
- Courage
- Waiting for the right time
- Resilience
- Testing of one's faith
- Resolving
- Self victory
- Last one standing
- Self-defensive
- Vigilance
- Commitment
- Discipline
- Self improvement
- Sensing danger
- Prepared

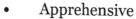

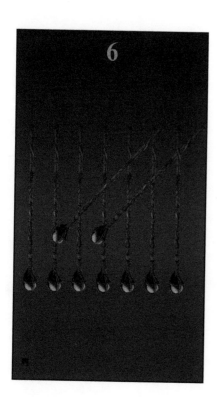

NEGATIVE ASPECTS

- Apprehensive
- Waiting for trouble to come in
- Feeling threatened
- More problems are coming
- Hastiness
- Unwilling to communicate
- Abandoned
- Lack of compromise
- An injury
- Sickness
- Delays
- Cancellations
- Taking a long time
- Nothing is going right
- Separation
- Disputes
- Returning to the battle field
- Failure to cross the finish line
- Lack of courage
- Stubbornness
- A chip on your shoulder
- No more fight within yourself
- On edge
- Lack of persistence

10 OF WANDS

CARD OF BURDEN

POSITIVE ASPECTS

- Tremendous responsibilities
- Building
- A lot of work
- Commitments
- Getting things done in a hurry
- Completion
- Can take on the pressure
- Great success
- Popularity
- Honesty
- Faith
- Self-confidence
- Will power
- Great responsibility
- Busy period is over
- Relief from stress
- Ambition
- Delegation
- Release
- Long term commitment
- An end of bad luck
- Prepared
- Sacrifices for success
- Honor
- Knowing you can do it

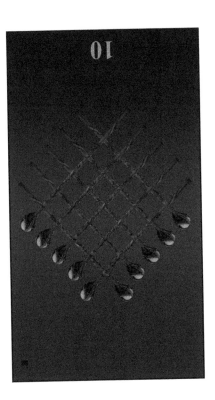

NEGATIVE ASPECTS

- Carrying a burden
- Can't see where you're going
- Weighed down with too many commitments and responsibilities
- Too much to handle all at once
- Lack of discipline
- Being involved in too many different areas
- Unfinished projects
- Can't see ahead in any areas
- Overload
- Fatigue
- Obstacles
- Insecurity
- Bad deal
- Sleepless nights
- No end in sight
- Working without rest
- Need for help
- Dodging your duties
- Misused skills
- Desire to control
- Betrayal
- Going astray
- Selfish goals

PAGE OF WANDS
CARD OF NEWS AND MESSAGES

POSITIVE ASPECTS

- Beginning a new project
- Growth
- Someone starting a new job
- News and messages
- Lots of information
- Learning a new area
- A surge of energy
- Business potential
- Doing surveying work
- Study of new interest
- New ideas
- Changing direction
- An apprenticeship
- Message from a near relative or a close friend
- Happy news is on the way
- A telephone call
- Word of mouth
- Cheerful
- Active
- Optimistic
- Fearless
- Charisma
- Extraverted
- Loveable rogue
- A survivor when things get tough

NEGATIVE ASPECTS

- Bad news
- Hasty
- Gullible
- Lack of ideas
- Lethargic
- Spoilt
- Pessimistic
- Lack of creativity
- Someone with bad intentions
- Childish behavior
- A loud mouth
- Self-conscious
- A trouble maker
- Boring
- Lack of action
- Instability
- Procrastinating
- Delinquent
- Lack of commitment
- Fake news
- A fraud
- Impatient
- Lack of energy
- Delayed news

KNIGHT OF WANDS
CARD OF VISITATION

POSITIVE ASPECTS

- A mature and energetic person
- Pushing forward
- Very strong bursting energy
- A sudden decision
- Acting quickly
- Doing something in the spare of the moment
- Visitors are coming
- A short a trip
- Starting new projects
- Self confidence
- Someone presenting ideas for business
- Moving on from one thing to another
- Changes of residence
- Adventurous
- Charming
- Fearless
- Motivated
- Bravery
- Confident
- A journey
- Passionate
- Power
- Artistic
- Talented
- Enthusiastic

NEGATIVE ASPECTS

- Someone who's too impulsive
- A lack of sureness
- Rushing into things too fast with out thought
- Not getting anywhere
- Someone's views trouble you
- A lack of self discipline
- Enthusiasm fizzles out
- Arrogant
- Overly confident
- Show off
- A loud mouth
- Violent
- Fearful
- Abusive
- A lack of enthusiasm
- Jealous
- Cancelled travel plans
- A lack of commitment
- Hastiness
- A separation
- Always coming and going
- Impulsiveness
- Delays
- A slack of ambition

QUEEN OF WANDS
CARD OF MANAGEMENT

POSITIVE ASPECTS

- A business woman
- Someone with lots of go
- A very generous, independent, and positive thinking person
- Someone who loves the domestic life
- A sexually attractive, warm and passionate person
- Someone with integrity
- A woman who is secure within herself
- Someone who is a boss, leader or manager
- A positive thinking person
- Someone with an attractive personality
- Strong
- Someone who enjoys motherhood
- Courageous
- Someone who is open to all people
- Optimistic
- Outgoing
- Someone who loves cats
- Efficient
- Generous
- Ambition
- Someone with a lot of experience in life
- Friendly
- Determination
- Vibrant
- Confident

NEGATIVE ASPECTS

- Another woman in mans life
- Playing with fire
- Stuck in the friend zone
- Pushy
- Demanding
- Overbearing
- A bully
- Unfriendly
- Jealous
- Manipulative
- Spiteful
- Deceitful
- Low confidence
- Unfaithful
- Hot tempered
- Fertility issues
- Bossiness
- Love of power status
- Greedy
- A cheater
- Untrustworthy
- Vengeful
- Gossiper
- Attention seeking

KING OF WANDS

CARD OF LEADERSHIP

POSITIVE ASPECTS

- A professional man with excellent leadership qualities
- Someone who is ready to get on with things and wants to do the work himself
- A positive, optimistic, strong and generous person
- A secure man in business
- Someone who is very honest and has no values in lies
- Excellent leadership qualities
- Someone who likes to be challenged
- Energetic
- Friendly
- Someone who is a boss, leader or manager
- Charming
- A way with words
- Fearless
- A natural leader
- Passionate
- Protective
- Sharpness
- Ambition
- Pride
- Progression
- Loyalty
- Self-confidence
- An entrepreneur
- A visionary

NEGATIVE ASPECTS

- Another man in a woman's life
- Playing with fire
- Someone who rushes into agreements before a final decision has been made
- Impulsiveness
- High expectations
- Arrogance
- A man of broken promises
- Hastiness
- Rude
- Forceful
- Abusive
- A bully
- Vicious
- Hot tempered
- Controlling
- Bitter
- Nasty
- Disloyal
- A womanizer
- Weak
- A tyrant
- Egotist
- A poor leader

SPREADS

Now that you've spent so much time learning about each card its time to now start putting your knowledge to the test with 5 different layout spread types. Each of the 5 spreads differentiate in difficultly, so take your time and do not rush in learning how they work best for you. Every individual will have their favorite type of spread which is the one that they can normally learn the fastest and/or the one they can relate to the best with their own interpretations and understandings. As you begin to understand and read the cards more confidently you will find that you'll be able to read the cards in your own unique way.

The most important rule I have before it comes to laying out your cards is how much time you spend shuffling your cards. Remember, the tarot cards are based on, and work off energy. The more time you spend shuffling the cards, the more energy you are putting through them I highly advise that you shuffle for a minimum of 1 minute or until you feel the need to stop shuffling there after.

PAST, PRESENT & FUTURE SPREAD

STEP 1: Shuffle your cards and divide your deck into 3 piles from left to right.
STEP 2: Starting from Pile 1 face up the first card from the pile.
Repeat for Piles 2 & 3 to reveal your cards.

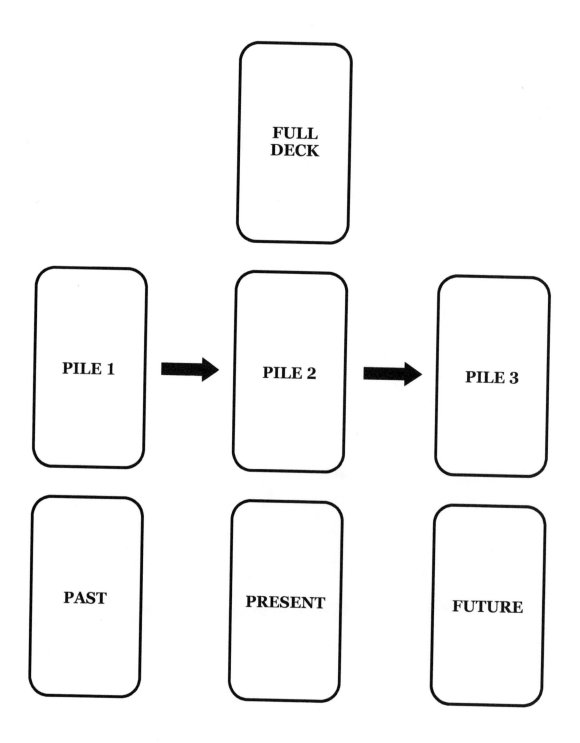

THE YES OR NO SPREAD
(Reading ACES only)

STEP 1: Shuffle the cards and divide your deck into 3 parts.
STEP 2: Starting from pile 1 draw out 13 cards only to see how many Aces you bring up then repeat the same process for piles 2 & 3. The legend below defines your answer to your question by the number of Aces that show within the 3 piles.

LEGEND:

No Ace: Is a definite No
1 Ace: Most probably No
2 Aces: Maybe
3 Aces: Almost definitely Yes
4 Aces: Is a definite Yes

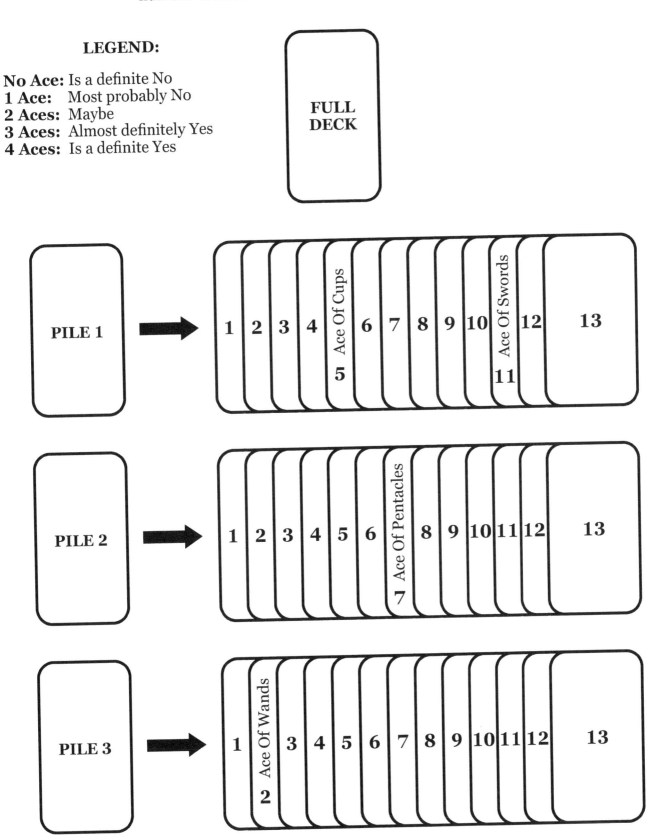

THE LOVE SPREAD

CARD 1: His/her story - What he/she is telling you.
CARD 2: What he/she is really thinking.
CARD 3: How he/she feels about you deep down.
CARD 4: How he/she is walking their truth.
CARD 5: Outsides influences on his/her talk.
CARD 6: How he/she will be walking their talk within 4-6 weeks.

```
          ┌─────┐
          │     │
          │  2  │
          │     │
          └─────┘

┌─────┐   ┌─────┐   ┌─────┐   ┌─────┐
│     │   │     │   │     │   │     │
│  1  │   │  4  │   │  5  │   │  6  │
│     │   │     │   │     │   │     │
└─────┘   └─────┘   └─────┘   └─────┘

          ┌─────┐
          │     │
          │  3  │
          │     │
          └─────┘
```

THE CELTIC CROSS SPREAD

CARD 1:   Influence directly affecting the querent.
CARD 2:   The opposing (act against) forces for good or evil
                  can accentuate or modify whatever the problem is.
CARD 3:   This is beneath the querent the basis of the matter
                  part of the subjects experience in the past.
CARD 4:   This is behind the querent the recent past in other words.
CARD 5:   Something that may happen in the future.
CARD 6:   This is before the querent or in the immediate future.
CARD 7:   Fears, negative feelings about the question.
CARD 8:   Family opinion, influence of family and friends.
CARD 9:   Any hopes and fears in the matter.
CARD 10:   The final outcome. This will include all cards.

THE PYRAMID SPREAD

CARDS 1-4:   Past.
CARD 5:   Culmination of past and beginning of present.
CARDS 6 -14:   Present.
CARDS 15 -18:   Future.
CARDS 19 - 20:   Obstacles/action.
CARD 21:   Outcome.

GROUP MEANINGS

Throughout the years of my Tarot reading experiences I have found many common card groupings that identify very important matters when doing my readings. These groupings are a combination of both positive and negative aspects but are the foundations of the main focus of the readings.

When you're able to identify these groupings, you can then work around them and put multiple stories together to find the solutions to either problems, blockages or acknowledge, achievements and successes as both types can also be seen depending of what types of energy you're seeing in the reading.

These groupings don't have to be all together in a reading but can come out in this exact formation depending on its urgency and/or how close the event is or was with its energy. Pay very close attention to every card in a reading and practice looking for these type of common combinations in your readings.

Success

Exams

Challenges

Ideas

Bank Manager or
Land & Property Owner

Health

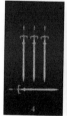   

Art, Creativity,
Music & Hobbies

Giving & or
Paying Debts

Doctor & or
Lawyer

Teacher Or Advisor

THE HIEROPHANT — THE HERMIT — THE HIGH PRIESTESS

Legal Matters

ACE Of Swords — JUSTICE — JUDGEMENT

Parting

2 — 5 — 8 — 3

Problems with Car

THE CHARIOT — THE MAGICIAN — THE DEVIL — ACE Of Swords

Sex

  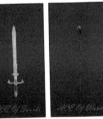

THE DEVIL — ACE Of Swords — ACE Of Wands

Power Or Passion — Phallic Symbol

Swindles, Mysteries & Lies

THE MOON — THE MAGICIAN — 7 — THE HIGH PRIESTESS — THE TOWER

Joy & Satisfaction

THE SUN — 10 — 9 — 6

Disappointment & Sadness

  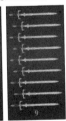 

4 — 5 — 9 — THE MOON

Muddles & Indecision

   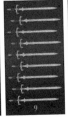 

THE CHARIOT — THE MOON — 7 — 9 — 2

Hard Work

7 — 10

Money & Security

PAGE PENTACLES

Making a Garden

THE EMPRESS

Parents Worry About You

THE MOON · THE EMPEROR · THE EMPRESS

Moving On

JUDGEMENT · THE FOOL · THE WORLD

A New Start Of Any Kind

THE FOOL · THE MAGICIAN · THE WHEEL OF FORTUNE · THE STAR · THE WORLD

Delay

THE HANGED MAN · THE HERMIT · 2

Victory

THE CHARIOT · THE SUN · JUSTICE · JUDGEMENT · THE WORLD

Food

THE EMPRESS

Marriage

THE HIEROPHANT · THE LOVERS · THE DEVIL

Commitment

Love & Romance

THE LOVERS

Loneliness & Being Happily Alone

  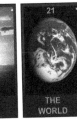

THE HERMIT — THE SUN — THE WORLD

Important Matters

THE FOOL — THE EMPEROR

Something You're Expecting

Psychic Inspiration

    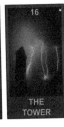    

THE MAGICIAN — THE HIGH PRIESTESS — THE HIEROPHANT — THE HERMIT — THE TOWER — THE STAR — THE MOON — THE DEVIL — ACE OF SWORDS

Reversed

Travel

KNIGHT OF SWORDS — KNIGHT OF WANDS — KNIGHT OF CUPS — KNIGHT OF PENTACLES — 6 — 8 — THE CHARIOT — THE SUN — THE WORLD

The Knights

Psychic Ability

THE HIGH PRIESTESS — THE MAGICIAN — THE HERMIT — THE MOON — ACE OF SWORDS

Holidays

THE SUN — THE EMPRESS — 6

A Warm Destination — The Country — A Cool Destination

Problems

7 — 9 — 8 — 9 — THE HANGED MAN

Engagement

ACE OF CUPS — 2 — 2

107

A New Enterprise & Self Employment

The Aces

Disappointing News

Substance Abuse

Alcohol Consumption

Cancelled Plans

A Windfall

A New Job

The Aces

Commitment

Endings of Any Kind

     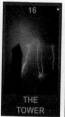   

Working Partnerships

2 Of Any Suit

THE LOVERS

Relevant Court Cards

KING of CUPS — QUEEN of CUPS — KING of SWORDS — QUEEN of SWORDS — KING of PENTACLES — QUEEN of PENTACLES — KING of WANDS — QUEEN of WANDS

Advice Given or Received

THE HIGH PRIESTESS — THE EMPEROR — THE HIEROPHANT — THE HERMIT — 7

The Kings & Queens

 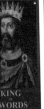    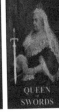  

KING of WANDS — KING of SWORDS — KING of PENTACLES — KING of CUPS — QUEEN of WANDS — QUEEN of SWORDS — QUEEN of PENTACLES — QUEEN of CUPS

Letters, News, Writing & Communications

The Pages

PAGE of WANDS — PAGE of SWORDS — PAGE of CUPS — PAGE of PENTACLES — 8 — ACE Of Wand — ACE Of Swords

Children

The Pages

PAGE of WANDS — PAGE of SWORDS — PAGE of CUPS — PAGE of PENTACLES — 6 — 10 — THE SUN

New House

THE EMPRESS   THE TOWER

With Land Or Garden Involved   A Problem With Property Or Loss Of Ones Home   Mortgage Difficulties

Diplomacy

STRENGTH   TEMPERANCE

Things being more or less than alright

A feeling of imprisonment or feeling trapped

THE DEVIL

A woman in a man's life

QUEEN CUPS   QUEEN PENTACLES   QUEEN WANDS   QUEEN SWORDS   THE HIGH PRIESTESS   THE EMPRESS   THE MOON

The Queens   If All Is Not Going Well

A man in a woman's life

The Kings

KING CUPS   KING PENTACLES   KING WANDS   KING SWORDS

KNIGHT CUPS   KNIGHT PENTACLES   KNIGHT WANDS   KNIGHT SWORDS   THE MAGICIAN   THE EMPEROR

The Knights

Printed in the USA
CPSIA information can be obtained
at www.ICGtesting.com
LVHW060018150624
783122LV00013B/131